MznLnx

Missing Links Exam Preps

Exam Prep for

Elementary Linear Algebra

Larson & Edwards & Falvo, 5th Edition

The MznLnx Exam Prep is your link from the texbook and lecture to your exams.
The MznLnx Exam Preps are unauthorized and comprehensive reviews of your textbooks.

All material provided by MznLnx and Rico Publications (c) 2010
Textbook publishers and textbook authors do not particpate in or contribute to these reviews.

MznLnx

Rico Publications

Exam Prep for Elementary Linear Algebra
5th Edition
Larson & Edwards & Falvo

Publisher: Raymond Houge
Assistant Editor: Michael Rouger
Text and Cover Designer: Lisa Buckner
Marketing Manager: Sara Swagger
Project Manager, Editorial Production: Jerry Emerson
Art Director: Vernon Lowerui

Product Manager: Dave Mason
Editorial Asitant: Rachel Guzmanji
Pedagogy: Debra Long
Cover Image: Jim Reed/Getty Images
Text and Cover Printer: City Printing, Inc.
Compositor: Media Mix, Inc.

(c) 2010 Rico Publications
ALL RIGHTS RESERVED. No part of this work covered by the copyright may be reproduced or used in any form or by an means--graphic, electronic, or mechanical, including photocopying, recording, taping, Web distribution, information storage, and retrieval systems, or in any other manner--without the written permission of the publisher.

Printed in the United States
ISBN:

For more information about our products, contact us at:
Dave.Mason@RicoPublications.com

For permission to use material from this text or product, submit a request online to:
Dave.Mason@RicoPublications.com

Contents

CHAPTER 1
SYSTEMS OF LINEAR EQUATIONS — 1

CHAPTER 2
MATRICES — 8

CHAPTER 3
DETERMINANTS — 22

CHAPTER 4
VECTOR SPACES — 37

CHAPTER 5
INNER PRODUCT SPACES — 48

CHAPTER 6
LINEAR TRANSFORMATIONS — 58

CHAPTER 7
EIGENVALUES AND EIGENVECTORS — 65

ANSWER KEY — 78

TO THE STUDENT

COMPREHENSIVE

The *MznLnx* Exam Prep series is designed to help you pass your exams. Editors at MznLnx review your textbooks and then prepare these practice exams to help you master the textbook material. Unlike study guides, workbooks, and practice tests provided by the texbook publisher and textbook authors, *MznLnx* gives you **all** of the material in each chapter in exam form, not just samples, so you can be sure to nail your exam.

MECHANICAL

The MznLnx Exam Prep series creates exams that will help you learn the subject matter as well as test you on your understanding. Each question is designed to help you master the concept. Just working through the exams, you gain an understanding of the subject--its a simple mechanical process that produces success.

INTEGRATED STUDY GUIDE AND REVIEW

MznLnx is not just a set of exams designed to test you, its also a comprehensive review of the subject content. Each exam question is also a review of the concept, making sure that you will get the answer correct without having to go to other sources of material. You learn as you go! Its the easiest way to pass an exam.

HUMOR

Studying can be tedious and dry. MznLnx's instructional design includes moderate humor within the exam questions on occassion, to break the tedium and revitalize the brain

Chapter 1. SYSTEMS OF LINEAR EQUATIONS

1. In mathematics, a _____ is a constant multiplicative factor of a certain object. For example, in the expression $9x^2$, the _____ of x^2 is 9.

   The object can be such things as a variable, a vector, a function, etc.

   a. Constant term
   b. Vandermonde polynomial
   c. Tschirnhaus transformation
   d. Coefficient

2. In mathematics, the _____ of a polynomial is the term of degree 0. For example, in the polynomial

   $X^3 + 2X + 3$

   over the variable X, the _____ is 3. Here, the _____ is given by a numeral, but it may also be specified by a letter that is a parameter rather than a variable, as in the polynomial

   $ax^2 + bx + c,$

   in the variable x, where a, b, and c are parameters so that c is the _____.

   a. Characteristic polynomial
   b. Quadratic function
   c. Constant term
   d. Symmetric polynomial

3. In algebra, a _____ is a function depending on n that associates a scalar, det(A), to an n×n square matrix A. The fundamental geometric meaning of a _____ is a scale factor for measure when A is regarded as a linear transformation. Determinants are important both in calculus, where they enter the substitution rule for several variables, and in multilinear algebra.

   For a fixed nonnegative integer n, there is a unique _____ function for the n×n matrices over any commutative ring R. In particular, this function exists when R is the field of real or complex numbers.

   a. Leibniz formula
   b. Functional determinant
   c. Pfaffian
   d. Determinant

Chapter 1. SYSTEMS OF LINEAR EQUATIONS

4. A _____ is a symbol that stands for a value that may vary; the term usually occurs in opposition to constant, which is a symbol for a non-varying value, i.e. completely fixed or fixed in the context of use. The concepts of constants and variables are fundamental to all modern mathematics, science, engineering, and computer programming.

Much of the basic theory for which we use variables today, such as school geometry and algebra, was developed thousands of years ago, but the use of symbolic formulae and variables is only several hundreds of years old.

   a. Variable
   b. -equivalence
   c. 2-bridge knot
   d. -module

5. In mathematics, a _____ is a collection of linear equations involving the same set of variables. For example,

$$3x + 2y - z = 1$$
$$2x - 2y + 4z = -2$$
$$-x + \tfrac{1}{2}y - z = 0$$

is a system of three equations in the three variables x, y, z. A solution to a linear system is an assignment of numbers to the variables such that all the equations are simultaneously satisfied.

   a. -module
   b. -equivalence
   c. Simultaneous equations
   d. System of linear equations

6. In mathematics, a _____ is a rectangular array of numbers. This way, matrices can record data that depend on multiple parameters. In particular they are used to keep track of the coefficients of multiple linear equations. Matrices are closely connected to linear transformations, which are higher-dimensional analogs of linear functions, i.e., functions of the form f(x) = c Â· x, where c is a constant. This map corresponds to a _____ with one row and column, with entry c. In addition to a number of elementary, entrywise operations such as _____ addition a key notion is _____ multiplication, which displays a number of features not encountered in numbers; for example, products of matrices depend on the order of the factors, unlike products of real numbers, say, where c Â· d = d Â· c for any two numbers c and d.

   a. Commutativity
   b. Matrix
   c. Heap
   d. Polynomial expression

Chapter 1. SYSTEMS OF LINEAR EQUATIONS

7. In linear algebra, _____ is an efficient algorithm for solving systems of linear equations, finding the rank of a matrix, and calculating the inverse of an invertible square matrix. _____ is named after German mathematician and scientist Carl Friedrich Gauss.

Elementary row operations are used to reduce a matrix to row echelon form.

   a. -module
   b. -equivalence
   c. Gaussian elimination
   d. 2-bridge knot

8. In its simplest meaning in mathematics and logic, an _____ is an action or procedure which produces a new value from one or more input values. There are two common types of operations: unary and binary. Unary operations involve only one value, such as negation and trigonometric functions.
   a. ADE classification
   b. Abelian P-root group
   c. Operation
   d. AKS primality test

9. In linear algebra, the _____ of a matrix A is the collection of cells $A_{i,j}$ where i is equal to j.

The _____ of a square matrix is the diagonal which runs from the top left corner to the bottom right corner. For example, the following matrix has 1s down its _____:

$$\begin{bmatrix} 1 & 0 & 0 \\ 0 & 1 & 0 \\ 0 & 0 & 1 \end{bmatrix}.$$

A square matrix like the above in which the entries outside the _____ are all zero is called a diagonal matrix.

   a. Complex Hadamard matrix
   b. Polynomial matrix
   c. Main diagonal
   d. Diagonalizable matrix

Chapter 1. SYSTEMS OF LINEAR EQUATIONS

10. In group theory, a branch of mathematics, the term _____ is used in two closely related senses:

    - the _____ of a group is its cardinality, i.e. the number of its elements;
    - the _____, sometimes period, of an element a of a group is the smallest positive integer m such that a^m = e (where e denotes the identity element of the group, and a^m denotes the product of m copies of a.) If no such m exists, we say that a has infinite _____. All elements of finite groups have finite _____.

We denote the _____ of a group G by ord(G) or $|G|$ and the _____ of an element a by ord(a) or $|a|$.

Example. The symmetric group S_3 has the following multiplication table.

This group has six elements, so ord(S_3) = 6.

   a. Outer automorphism group
   b. Artin group
   c. Index calculus algorithm
   d. Order

11. In abstract algebra and algebraic geometry, the _____ of a commutative ring R, denoted by Spec(R), is the set of all proper prime ideals of R. It is commonly augmented with the Zariski topology and with a structure sheaf, turning it into a locally ringed space.

Spec(R) can be turned into a topological space as follows: a subset V of Spec(R) is closed if and only if there exists a subset I of R such that V consists of all those prime ideals in R that contain I. This is called the Zariski topology on Spec(R.)

Spec(R) is a compact space, but almost never Hausdorff: in fact, the maximal ideals in R are precisely the closed points in this topology.

   a. Spectrum
   b. Krull dimension
   c. Hilbert polynomial
   d. Discrete valuation

12. In linear algebra, the _____ of a matrix is obtained by changing a matrix in some way.

Given the matrices A and B, where:

$$A = \begin{bmatrix} 1 & 3 & 2 \\ 2 & 0 & 1 \\ 5 & 2 & 2 \end{bmatrix}, \quad B = \begin{bmatrix} 4 \\ 3 \\ 1 \end{bmatrix}$$

Then, the _____ is written as:

$$(A|B) = \begin{bmatrix} 1 & 3 & 2 & 4 \\ 2 & 0 & 1 & 3 \\ 5 & 2 & 2 & 1 \end{bmatrix}$$

This is useful when solving systems of linear equations or the _____ may also be used to find the inverse of a matrix by combining it with the identity matrix.

Let C be a square 2×2 matrix where
$$C = \begin{bmatrix} 1 & 3 \\ -5 & 0 \end{bmatrix}$$

To find the inverse of C we create (C | I) where I is the 2×2 identity matrix.

a. Unistochastic matrix
b. Unitary matrix
c. Euclidean distance matrix
d. Augmented matrix

13. In linear algebra, the _____ refers to a matrix consisting of the coefficients of the variables in a set of linear equations.

In general, a system with m linear equations and n unknowns can be written as

$$a_{11}x_1 + a_{12}x_2 + ... + a_{1n}x_n = b_1$$
$$a_{21}x_1 + a_{22}x_2 + ... + a_{2n}x_n = b_2$$
$$\vdots$$
$$a_{m1}x_1 + a_{m2}x_2 + ... + a_{mn}x_n = b_m$$

where $x_1, x_2, ..., x_n$ are the unknowns and the numbers $a_{11}, a_{12}, ..., a_{mn}$ are the coefficients of the system. The _____ is the mxn matrix with the coefficient a_{ij} as the (i,j)-th entry:

$$\begin{bmatrix} a_{11} & a_{12} & \cdots & a_{1n} \\ a_{21} & a_{22} & \cdots & a_{2n} \\ \vdots & \vdots & \ddots & \vdots \\ a_{m1} & a_{m2} & \cdots & a_{mn} \end{bmatrix}$$

a. Linear inequality
b. Segre classification
c. Centrosymmetric matrix
d. Coefficient matrix

14. In mathematics, a _____ is a function on a group of a special form, which depends on a linear representation of the group and additional data. For the case of a finite group, matrix coefficients express the action of the elements of the group in the specified representation via the entries of the corresponding matrices.

Matrix coefficients of representations of Lie groups turned out to be intimately related with the theory of special functions, providing a unifying approach to large parts of this theory.

a. Dual representation
b. Gelfand pair
c. Tempered representation
d. Matrix coefficient

15. A _____ is a mathematical equation for an unknown function of one or several variables that relates the values of the function itself and its derivatives of various orders. Differential equations play a prominent role in engineering, physics, economics and other disciplines. Visualization of airflow into a duct modelled using the Navier-Stokes equations, a set of partial differential equations.

Differential equations arise in many areas of science and technology; whenever a deterministic relationship involving some continuously changing quantities (modeled by functions) and their rates of change (expressed as derivatives) is known or postulated.

a. -module
b. 2-bridge knot
c. -equivalence
d. Differential equation

16. In mathematics, a system of linear equations is considered _____ if there are more equations than unknowns. The terminology can be described in terms of the concept of counting constants. Each unknown can be seen as an available degree of freedom.
    a. Elementary matrix
    b. Orthogonalization
    c. Euclidean subspace
    d. Overdetermined

Chapter 2. MATRICES

1. _____ is the mathematical process of putting things together. The plus sign '+' means that numbers are added together. For example, in the picture on the right, there are 3 + 2 apples--meaning three apples and two other apples--which is the same as five apples, since 3 + 2 = 5.

    a. Abelian P-root group
    b. ADE classification
    c. AKS primality test
    d. Addition

2. In mathematics, a _____ is a rectangular array of numbers. This way, matrices can record data that depend on multiple parameters. In particular they are used to keep track of the coefficients of multiple linear equations. Matrices are closely connected to linear transformations, which are higher-dimensional analogs of linear functions, i.e., functions of the form f(x) = c Â· x, where c is a constant. This map corresponds to a _____ with one row and column, with entry c. In addition to a number of elementary, entrywise operations such as _____ addition a key notion is _____ multiplication, which displays a number of features not encountered in numbers; for example, products of matrices depend on the order of the factors, unlike products of real numbers, say, where c Â· d = d Â· c for any two numbers c and d.

    a. Heap
    b. Matrix
    c. Commutativity
    d. Polynomial expression

3. The real component of a quaternion is also called its _____ part.

The term is also sometimes used informally to mean a vector, matrix, tensor, or other usually 'compound' value that is actually reduced to a single component. Thus, for example, the product of a 1×n matrix and an n×1 matrix, which is formally a 1×1 matrix, is often said to be a _____.

    a. Self-adjoint
    b. Tensor product
    c. Distributivity
    d. Scalar

4. In linear algebra, the _____ of a matrix A is the collection of cells $A_{i,j}$ where i is equal to j.

The _____ of a square matrix is the diagonal which runs from the top left corner to the bottom right corner. For example, the following matrix has 1s down its _____:

$$\begin{bmatrix} 1 & 0 & 0 \\ 0 & 1 & 0 \\ 0 & 0 & 1 \end{bmatrix}.$$

Chapter 2. MATRICES 9

A square matrix like the above in which the entries outside the _____ are all zero is called a diagonal matrix.

   a. Diagonalizable matrix
   b. Polynomial matrix
   c. Complex Hadamard matrix
   d. Main diagonal

5. In mathematics, a _____ is a constant multiplicative factor of a certain object. For example, in the expression $9x^2$, the _____ of x^2 is 9.

The object can be such things as a variable, a vector, a function, etc.

   a. Tschirnhaus transformation
   b. Constant term
   c. Coefficient
   d. Vandermonde polynomial

6. In mathematics and group theory, a _____ system for the action of a group G on a set X is a partition of X that is G-invariant. In terms of the associated equivalence relation on X, G-invariance means that

   $x \equiv y$ implies $gx \equiv gy$

for all g in G and all x, y in X. The action of G on X determines a natural action of G on any _____ system for X.

Each element of the _____ system is called a _____.

   a. Parker vector
   b. Frobenius group
   c. Symmetric group
   d. Block

7. In mathematics the _____ of a set which is equipped with the operation of addition is an element which, when added to any element x in the set, yields x. One of the most familiar additive identities is the number 0 from elementary mathematics, but additive identities occur in other mathematical structures where addition is defined, such as in groups and rings.

   - The _____ familiar from elementary mathematics is zero, denoted 0. For example,

$5 + 0 = 5 = 0 + 5.$

- In the natural numbers N and all of its supersets (the integers Z, the rational numbers Q, the real numbers R, or the complex numbers C), the _____ is 0. Thus for any one of these numbers n,

$n + 0 = n = 0 + n.$

Let N be a set which is closed under the operation of addition, denoted +. An _____ for N is any element e such that for any element n in N,

$e + n = n = n + e.$

a. Identity element
b. Universal algebra
c. External
d. Additive identity

8. In mathematics, the _____ of a number n is the number that, when added to n, yields zero. The _____ of F is denoted −F.

For example, the _____ of 7 is −7, because 7 + (−7) = 0, and the _____ of −0.3 is 0.3, because −0.3 + 0.3 = 0.

a. Additive inverse
b. Interior algebra
c. Artinian ideal
d. Isomorphism class

9. where B is the _____ of the product. To remove A_1 from the product, we can then write

$$A_1^{-1}(A_1 A_2 \cdots A_n)B = A_1^{-1}I$$

which would reduce the equation to

$$(A_2 A_3 \cdots A_n)B = A_1^{-1}I.$$

Likewise, then, from

$$A_2^{-1}(A_2 A_3 \cdots A_n)B = A_2^{-1}A_1^{-1}I$$

which simplifies to

$$(A_3 A_4 \cdots A_n)B = A_2^{-1}A_1^{-1}I.$$

If one repeat the process up to A_n, the equation becomes

$$B = A_n^{-1}A_{n-1}^{-1} \cdots A_2^{-1}A_1^{-1}I$$

$$B = A_n^{-1}A_{n-1}^{-1} \cdots A_2^{-1}A_1^{-1}$$

but B is the _____, i.e. $B = (A_1 A_2 \cdots A_n)^{-1}$ so the property is established.

Over the field of real numbers, the set of singular n-by-n matrices, considered as a subset of $R^{n \times n}$, is a null set, i.e., has Lebesgue measure zero.

a. AKS primality test
b. ADE classification
c. Abelian P-root group
d. Inverse matrix

10.   In mathematics, _____ is the operation of adding two matrices by adding the corresponding entries together. However, there is another operation which could also be considered as a kind of addition for matrices.

The usual _____ is defined for two matrices of the same dimensions.

a. Nonlinear eigenproblem
b. Projection-valued measure
c. Cofactor
d. Matrix addition

11.   In mathematics, _____ is one of the basic operations defining a vector space in linear algebra Note that _____ is different from scalar product which is an inner product between two vectors.

Chapter 2. MATRICES

More specifically, if K is a field and V is a vector space over K, then _____ is a function from K × V to V. The result of applying this function to c in K and v in V is denoted cv.

a. Symplectic vector space
b. K-frame
c. Scalar multiplication
d. Matrix pencil

12. In mathematics, particularly linear algebra, a _____ is a matrix with all its entries being zero. Some examples of zero matrices are

$$0_{1,1} = \begin{bmatrix} 0 \end{bmatrix}, \quad 0_{2,2} = \begin{bmatrix} 0 & 0 \\ 0 & 0 \end{bmatrix}, \quad 0_{2,3} = \begin{bmatrix} 0 & 0 & 0 \\ 0 & 0 & 0 \end{bmatrix},$$

The set of m×n matrices with entries in a ring K forms a ring $K_{m,n}$. The _____ $0_{K_{m,n}}$ in $K_{m,n}$ is the matrix with all entries equal to 0_K, where 0_K is the additive identity in K.

a. Regular Hadamard matrix
b. Complex Hadamard matrix
c. Normal matrix
d. Zero matrix

13. In linear algebra, the _____ or unit matrix of size n is the n-by-n square matrix with ones on the main diagonal and zeros elsewhere. It is denoted by I_n, or simply by I if the size is immaterial or can be trivially determined by the context. (In some fields, such as quantum mechanics, the _____ is denoted by a boldface one, 1; otherwise it is identical to I.)

a. Identity matrix
b. Associativity
c. Artinian ideal
d. Orthogonal

14. In group theory, a branch of mathematics, the term _____ is used in two closely related senses:

- the _____ of a group is its cardinality, i.e. the number of its elements;
- the _____, sometimes period, of an element a of a group is the smallest positive integer m such that a^m = e (where e denotes the identity element of the group, and a^m denotes the product of m copies of a.) If no such m exists, we say that a has infinite _____. All elements of finite groups have finite _____.

We denote the _____ of a group G by ord(G) or $|G|$ and the _____ of an element a by ord(a) or $|a|$.

Example. The symmetric group S_3 has the following multiplication table.

This group has six elements, so ord(S_3) = 6.

   a. Outer automorphism group
   b. Artin group
   c. Index calculus algorithm
   d. Order

15. In linear algebra, the _____ of a matrix A is another matrix A^T (also written A', A^{tr} or ^tA) created by any one of the following equivalent actions:

- write the rows of A as the columns of A^T
- write the columns of A as the rows of A^T
- reflect A by its main diagonal (which starts from the top left) to obtain A^T

Formally, the _____ of an m × n matrix A with elements A_{ij} is the n × m matrix

$$A^T_{ij} = A_{ji} \text{ for } 1 \leq i \leq n, 1 \leq j \leq m.$$

The _____ of a scalar is the same scalar.

- $\begin{bmatrix} 1 & 2 \end{bmatrix}^T = \begin{bmatrix} 1 \\ 2 \end{bmatrix}.$

- $\begin{bmatrix} 1 & 2 \\ 3 & 4 \end{bmatrix}^T = \begin{bmatrix} 1 & 3 \\ 2 & 4 \end{bmatrix}.$

- $\begin{bmatrix} 1 & 2 \\ 3 & 4 \\ 5 & 6 \end{bmatrix}^T = \begin{bmatrix} 1 & 3 & 5 \\ 2 & 4 & 6 \end{bmatrix}.$

For matrices A, B and scalar c we have the following properties of _____:

1. $\left(\mathbf{A}^\mathrm{T}\right)^\mathrm{T} = \mathbf{A}$

   Taking the _____ is an involution (self inverse.)

- $(\mathbf{A} + \mathbf{B})^\mathrm{T} = \mathbf{A}^\mathrm{T} + \mathbf{B}^\mathrm{T}$

   The _____ respects addition.

- $(\mathbf{AB})^\mathrm{T} = \mathbf{B}^\mathrm{T}\mathbf{A}^\mathrm{T}$

   Note that the order of the factors reverses. From this one can deduce that a square matrix A is invertible if and only if A^T is invertible, and in this case we have $(A^{-1})^T = (A^T)^{-1}$. It is relatively easy to extend this result to the general case of multiple matrices, where we find that $(ABC...XYZ)^T = Z^T Y^T X^T ... C^T B^T A^T$.

- $(c\mathbf{A})^\mathrm{T} = c\mathbf{A}^\mathrm{T}$

   The _____ of a scalar is the same scalar. Together with (2), this states that the _____ is a linear map from the space of m × n matrices to the space of all n × m matrices.

- $\det(\mathbf{A}^\mathrm{T}) = \det(\mathbf{A})$

   The determinant of a square matrix is the same as that of its _____.

- The dot product of two column vectors a and b can be computed as

   $$\mathbf{a} \cdot \mathbf{b} = \mathbf{a}^\mathrm{T} \mathbf{b},$$

which is written as $a_i\, b^i$ in Einstein notation.
- If A has only real entries, then $A^T A$ is a positive-semidefinite matrix.
- $\left(\mathbf{A}^\mathrm{T}\right)^{-1} = \left(\mathbf{A}^{-1}\right)^\mathrm{T}$

   The _____ of an invertible matrix is also invertible, and its inverse is the _____ of the inverse of the original matrix.

- If A is a square matrix, then its eigenvalues are equal to the eigenvalues of its _____.

A square matrix whose _____ is equal to itself is called a symmetric matrix; that is, A is symmetric if

$$\mathbf{A}^T = \mathbf{A}.$$

A square matrix whose _____ is also its inverse is called an orthogonal matrix; that is, G is orthogonal if

$$\mathbf{G}\mathbf{G}^T = \mathbf{G}^T\mathbf{G} = \mathbf{I}_n,$$ the identity matrix, i.e. $G^T = G^{-1}$.

A square matrix whose _____ is equal to its negative is called skew-symmetric matrix; that is, A is skew-symmetric if

$$\mathbf{A}^T = -\mathbf{A}.$$

The conjugate _____ of the complex matrix A, written as A*, is obtained by taking the _____ of A and the complex conjugate of each entry:

$$\mathbf{A}^* = (\overline{\mathbf{A}})^T = \overline{(\mathbf{A}^T)}.$$

If f: V→W is a linear map between vector spaces V and W with nondegenerate bilinear forms, we define the _____ of f to be the linear map $^t f$: W→V, determined by

$$B_V(v, {}^t f(w)) = B_W(f(v), w) \quad \forall\ v \in V, w \in W.$$

Here, B_V and B_W are the bilinear forms on V and W respectively. The matrix of the _____ of a map is the transposed matrix only if the bases are orthonormal with respect to their bilinear forms.

Over a complex vector space, one often works with sesquilinear forms instead of bilinear (conjugate-linear in one argument.)

   a. Drazin inverse
   b. Tridiagonal matrix
   c. Levinson recursion
   d. Transpose

16. In mathematics, a _____ is a collection of linear equations involving the same set of variables. For example,

$$3x + 2y - z = 1$$
$$2x - 2y + 4z = -2$$
$$-x + \tfrac{1}{2}y - z = 0$$

is a system of three equations in the three variables x, y, z. A solution to a linear system is an assignment of numbers to the variables such that all the equations are simultaneously satisfied.

a. -module
b. System of linear equations
c. Simultaneous equations
d. -equivalence

17. Let S be a set with a binary operation * . If e is an identity element of (S, *) and a * b = e, then a is called a _____ of b and b is called a right inverse of a. If an element x is both a _____ and a right inverse of y, then x is called a two-sided inverse, or simply an inverse, of y.
  a. -module
  b. -equivalence
  c. 2-bridge knot
  d. Left inverse

18. If $A_1, A_2, ..., A_n$ are _____ square matrices over a field, then

$$(\mathbf{A}_1 \mathbf{A}_2 \cdots \mathbf{A}_n)^{-1} = \mathbf{A}_n^{-1} \mathbf{A}_{n-1}^{-1} \cdots \mathbf{A}_1^{-1}.$$

It becomes evident why this is the case if one attempts to find an inverse for the product of the A_is from first principles, that is, that we wish to determine B such that

$$(\mathbf{A}_1 \mathbf{A}_2 \cdots \mathbf{A}_n)\mathbf{B} = \mathbf{I}$$

where B is the inverse matrix of the product. To remove A_1 from the product, we can then write

$$\mathbf{A}_1^{-1}(\mathbf{A}_1 \mathbf{A}_2 \cdots \mathbf{A}_n)\mathbf{B} = \mathbf{A}_1^{-1}\mathbf{I}$$

Chapter 2. MATRICES

which would reduce the equation to

$$(A_2 A_3 \cdots A_n)B = A_1^{-1} I.$$

Likewise, then, from

$$A_2^{-1}(A_2 A_3 \cdots A_n)B = A_2^{-1} A_1^{-1} I$$

which simplifies to

$$(A_3 A_4 \cdots A_n)B = A_2^{-1} A_1^{-1} I.$$

If one repeat the process up to A_n, the equation becomes

$$B = A_n^{-1} A_{n-1}^{-1} \cdots A_2^{-1} A_1^{-1} I$$

$$B = A_n^{-1} A_{n-1}^{-1} \cdots A_2^{-1} A_1^{-1}$$

but B is the inverse matrix, i.e. $B = (A_1 A_2 \cdots A_n)^{-1}$ so the property is established.

Over the field of real numbers, the set of singular n-by-n matrices, considered as a subset of $R^{n \times n}$, is a null set, i.e., has Lebesgue measure zero.

   a. -equivalence
   b. -module
   c. 2-bridge knot
   d. Nonsingular

19. In mathematics, a _____ is a function between two vector spaces that preserves the operations of vector addition and scalar multiplication. The expression 'linear operator' is in especially common use, for linear maps from a vector space to itself In advanced mathematics, the definition of linear function coincides with the definition of _____.
   a. Real matrices
   b. Rotation
   c. Homomorphic secret sharing
   d. Linear map

20. for some m×n matrix A, called the _____ of T.

Chapter 2. MATRICES

Matrices allow arbitrary linear transformations to be represented in a consistent format, suitable for computation. This also allows transformations to be concatenated easily (by multiplying their matrices.)

a. -equivalence
b. -module
c. 2-bridge knot
d. Transformation matrix

21. In its simplest meaning in mathematics and logic, an _____ is an action or procedure which produces a new value from one or more input values. There are two common types of operations: unary and binary. Unary operations involve only one value, such as negation and trigonometric functions.
    a. AKS primality test
    b. Operation
    c. Abelian P-root group
    d. ADE classification

22. In mathematics, a _____, probability matrix, or transition matrix is used to describe the transitions of a Markov chain. It has found use in probability theory, statistics and linear algebra, as well as computer science. There are several different definitions and types of stochastic matrices;

    A right _____ is a square matrix each of whose rows consists of nonnegative real numbers, with each row summing to 1.

    a. Bisymmetric matrix
    b. Permutation matrix
    c. Supermatrix
    d. Stochastic matrix

23. In abstract algebra and algebraic geometry, the _____ of a commutative ring R, denoted by Spec(R), is the set of all proper prime ideals of R. It is commonly augmented with the Zariski topology and with a structure sheaf, turning it into a locally ringed space.

Spec(R) can be turned into a topological space as follows: a subset V of Spec(R) is closed if and only if there exists a subset I of R such that V consists of all those prime ideals in R that contain I. This is called the Zariski topology on Spec(R.)

Spec(R) is a compact space, but almost never Hausdorff: in fact, the maximal ideals in R are precisely the closed points in this topology.

Chapter 2. MATRICES

a. Discrete valuation
b. Krull dimension
c. Spectrum
d. Hilbert polynomial

24. Economics is the social science that studies the production, distribution, and consumption of goods and services. The term economics comes from the Ancient Greek oá¼°κονομῖα from oá¼¶κος (oikos, 'house') + vÏŒμος (nomos, 'custom' or 'law'), hence 'rules of the house(hold)'. Current _____ models developed out of the broader field of political economy in the late 19th century, owing to a desire to use an empirical approach more akin to the physical sciences.

a. AKS primality test
b. Economic
c. Abelian P-root group
d. ADE classification

25. The term _____ is useful for describing certain algebraic structures. The term comes from the concept of an _____ binary operation which is a binary operation that draws from some _____ set. To be more specific, a left _____ binary operation on S over R is a function $f : R \times S \to S$ and a right _____ binary operation on S over R is a function $f : S \times R \to S$ where S is the set the operation is defined on, and R is the _____ set (the set the operation is defined over.)

a. Unit ring
b. Algebraic structure
c. External
d. Orthogonal

26. The method of _____ is used to approximately solve overdetermined systems, i.e. systems of equations in which there are more equations than unknowns. _____ is often applied in statistical contexts, particularly regression analysis.

_____ can be interpreted as a method of fitting data.

a. Least squares
b. -equivalence
c. 2-bridge knot
d. -module

27. In geometry, a _____ is a straight curve. When geometry is used to model the real world, lines are used to represent straight objects with negligible width and height. Lines are an idealisation of such objects and have no width or height at all and are usually considered to be infinitely long.

Chapter 2. MATRICES

a. Line
b. -module
c. -equivalence
d. 2-bridge knot

28. In mathematics, an element x of a ring R is called _____ if there exists some positive integer n such that x^n = 0.

The term was introduced by Benjamin Peirce in the context of elements of an algebra that vanish when raised to a power.

- This definition can be applied in particular to square matrices. The matrix

$$A = \begin{pmatrix} 0 & 1 & 0 \\ 0 & 0 & 1 \\ 0 & 0 & 0 \end{pmatrix}$$

is _____ because A^3 = 0. See _____ matrix for more.

a. Hochschild homology
b. Nilpotent
c. Product ring
d. Ring of integers

29. In linear algebra, a _____ is a square matrix N such that

$$N^k = 0$$

for some positive integer k. The smallest such k is sometimes called the degree of N.

More generally, a nilpotent transformation is a linear transformation L of a vector space such that L^k = 0 for some positive integer k.

a. Shift matrix
b. Main diagonal
c. Pascal matrix
d. Nilpotent matrix

30. In mathematics, specifically group theory, the _____ of a subgroup H in a group G is the e;relative sizee; of H in G. For example, if H has _____ 2 in G, then intuitively e;halfe; of the elements of G lie in H. The _____ of H in G is usually denoted $|G:H|$ or $[G:H]$.

If G and H are finite groups, then the _____ of H in G is simply the quotient of the orders of the two groups:

$$|G:H| = \frac{|G|}{|H|}.$$

By Lagrange's theorem, this number is always a positive integer.

If G and H are infinite, then the _____ of H is G is defined as the number of cosets of H in G.

a. Outer automorphism
b. Index
c. Inner automorphism
d. Even permutations

Chapter 3. DETERMINANTS

1. In algebra, a _____ is a function depending on n that associates a scalar, det(A), to an n×n square matrix A. The fundamental geometric meaning of a _____ is a scale factor for measure when A is regarded as a linear transformation. Determinants are important both in calculus, where they enter the substitution rule for several variables, and in multilinear algebra.

For a fixed nonnegative integer n, there is a unique _____ function for the n×n matrices over any commutative ring R. In particular, this function exists when R is the field of real or complex numbers.

   a. Leibniz formula
   b. Pfaffian
   c. Functional determinant
   d. Determinant

2. In mathematics, a _____ is a rectangular array of numbers. This way, matrices can record data that depend on multiple parameters. In particular they are used to keep track of the coefficients of multiple linear equations. Matrices are closely connected to linear transformations, which are higher-dimensional analogs of linear functions, i.e., functions of the form f(x) = c · x, where c is a constant. This map corresponds to a _____ with one row and column, with entry c. In addition to a number of elementary, entrywise operations such as _____ addition a key notion is _____ multiplication, which displays a number of features not encountered in numbers; for example, products of matrices depend on the order of the factors, unlike products of real numbers, say, where c · d = d · c for any two numbers c and d.
   a. Commutativity
   b. Matrix
   c. Heap
   d. Polynomial expression

3. In linear algebra, the _____ describes a particular construction that is useful for calculating both the determinant and inverse of square matrices. Specifically the _____ of the (i, j) entry of a matrix, also known as the (i, j) _____ of that matrix, is the signed minor of that entry.

Finding the minors of a matrix A is a multi-step process:

   1. Choose an entry a_{ij} from the matrix.
   2. Cross out the entries that lie in the corresponding row i and column j.
   3. Rewrite the matrix without the marked entries.
   4. Obtain the determinant M_{ij} of this new matrix.

M_{ij} is termed the minor for entry a_{ij}.

Chapter 3. DETERMINANTS

If i + j is an even number, the _____ C_{ij} of a_{ij} coincides with its minor:

$$C_{ij} = M_{ij}.$$

Otherwise, it is equal to the additive inverse of its minor:

$$C_{ij} = -M_{ij}.$$

If A is a square matrix, then the minor of its entry a_{ij}, also known as the i,j, or (i,j), or (i,j)th minor of A, is denoted by M_{ij} and is defined to be the determinant of the submatrix obtained by removing from A its i-th row and j-th column.

   a. Resolvent set
   b. Complex structure
   c. Coefficient matrix
   d. Cofactor

4. In linear algebra, a _____ of a matrix A is the determinant of some smaller square matrix, cut down from A by removing one or more of its rows or columns. Minors obtained by removing just one row and one column from square matrices (first minors) are required for calculating matrix cofactors, which in turn are useful for computing both the determinant and inverse of square matrices.
   a. Rng
   b. Minor
   c. Supergroup
   d. Purification

5. In linear algebra, the _____ of a matrix A is the collection of cells $A_{i,j}$ where i is equal to j.

The _____ of a square matrix is the diagonal which runs from the top left corner to the bottom right corner. For example, the following matrix has 1s down its _____:

$$\begin{bmatrix} 1 & 0 & 0 \\ 0 & 1 & 0 \\ 0 & 0 & 1 \end{bmatrix}.$$

A square matrix like the above in which the entries outside the _____ are all zero is called a diagonal matrix.

a. Complex Hadamard matrix
b. Diagonalizable matrix
c. Main diagonal
d. Polynomial matrix

6. In mathematics, an _____ of a product of sums expresses it as a sum of products by using the fact that multiplication distributes over addition. Expansions of polynomials are obtained by multiplying together their factors, which results in a sum of terms with variables raised to different degrees.

To multiply two factors, each term of the first factor must be multiplied by each term of the other factor.

a. Equipotential surfaces
b. Analytic subgroup
c. Expansion
d. Ordered vector space

7. In linear algebra, a _____ is a square matrix in which the entries outside the main diagonal (â†") are all zero. The diagonal entries themselves may or may not be zero. Thus, the matrix D = ($d_{i,j}$) with n columns and n rows is diagonal if:

$$d_{i,j} = 0 \text{ if } i \neq j \qquad \forall i,j \in \{1, 2, \ldots, n\}.$$

For example, the following matrix is diagonal:

$$\begin{bmatrix} 1 & 0 & 0 \\ 0 & 4 & 0 \\ 0 & 0 & -3 \end{bmatrix}.$$

The term _____ may sometimes refer to a rectangular _____, which is an m-by-n matrix with only the entries of the form $d_{i,i}$ possibly non-zero; for example,

$$\begin{bmatrix} 1 & 0 & 0 \\ 0 & 4 & 0 \\ 0 & 0 & -3 \\ 0 & 0 & 0 \end{bmatrix}, \text{ or}$$

a. Matrix representation
b. Levinson recursion
c. Hessenberg matrix
d. Diagonal matrix

8. In the mathematical discipline of linear algebra, a _____ is a special kind of square matrix where the entries either below or above the main diagonal are zero. Because matrix equations with triangular matrices are easier to solve they are very important in numerical analysis. The LU decomposition gives an algorithm to decompose any invertible matrix A into a normed lower triangle matrix L and an upper triangle matrix U.

a. Hilbert matrix
b. Diagonally dominant
c. Triangular matrix
d. Circulant matrix

9. In its simplest meaning in mathematics and logic, an _____ is an action or procedure which produces a new value from one or more input values. There are two common types of operations: unary and binary. Unary operations involve only one value, such as negation and trigonometric functions.

a. Abelian P-root group
b. Operation
c. ADE classification
d. AKS primality test

10. The real component of a quaternion is also called its _____ part.

The term is also sometimes used informally to mean a vector, matrix, tensor, or other usually 'compound' value that is actually reduced to a single component. Thus, for example, the product of a 1×n matrix and an n×1 matrix, which is formally a 1×1 matrix, is often said to be a _____.

a. Tensor product
b. Self-adjoint
c. Distributivity
d. Scalar

11. Let S be a set with a binary operation * . If e is an identity element of (S, *) and a * b = e, then a is called a _____ of b and b is called a right inverse of a. If an element x is both a _____ and a right inverse of y, then x is called a two-sided inverse, or simply an inverse, of y.

Chapter 3. DETERMINANTS

   a. 2-bridge knot
   b. -equivalence
   c. -module
   d. Left inverse

12. Matrix inversion is the process of finding the matrix B that satisfies the prior equation for a given _____ A.
   a. Independent equation
   b. Invertible matrix
   c. Overdetermined
   d. Orientation

13. In mathematics, a _____ is a function between two vector spaces that preserves the operations of vector addition and scalar multiplication. The expression 'linear operator' is in especially common use, for linear maps from a vector space to itself In advanced mathematics, the definition of linear function coincides with the definition of _____.
   a. Linear map
   b. Real matrices
   c. Rotation
   d. Homomorphic secret sharing

14. where B is the _____ of the product. To remove A_1 from the product, we can then write

$$\mathbf{A}_1^{-1}(\mathbf{A}_1\mathbf{A}_2\cdots\mathbf{A}_n)\mathbf{B} = \mathbf{A}_1^{-1}\mathbf{I}$$

which would reduce the equation to

$$(\mathbf{A}_2\mathbf{A}_3\cdots\mathbf{A}_n)\mathbf{B} = \mathbf{A}_1^{-1}\mathbf{I}.$$

Likewise, then, from

$$\mathbf{A}_2^{-1}(\mathbf{A}_2\mathbf{A}_3\cdots\mathbf{A}_n)\mathbf{B} = \mathbf{A}_2^{-1}\mathbf{A}_1^{-1}\mathbf{I}$$

which simplifies to

$$(\mathbf{A}_3\mathbf{A}_4\cdots\mathbf{A}_n)\mathbf{B} = \mathbf{A}_2^{-1}\mathbf{A}_1^{-1}\mathbf{I}.$$

Chapter 3. DETERMINANTS

If one repeat the process up to A_n, the equation becomes

$$B = A_n^{-1} A_{n-1}^{-1} \cdots A_2^{-1} A_1^{-1} I$$

$$B = A_n^{-1} A_{n-1}^{-1} \cdots A_2^{-1} A_1^{-1}$$

but B is the _____, i.e. $B = (A_1 A_2 \cdots A_n)^{-1}$ so the property is established.

Over the field of real numbers, the set of singular n-by-n matrices, considered as a subset of $R^{n \times n}$, is a null set, i.e., has Lebesgue measure zero.

   a. ADE classification
   b. Inverse matrix
   c. Abelian P-root group
   d. AKS primality test

15. If $A_1, A_2, ..., A_n$ are _____ square matrices over a field, then

$$(A_1 A_2 \cdots A_n)^{-1} = A_n^{-1} A_{n-1}^{-1} \cdots A_1^{-1}.$$

It becomes evident why this is the case if one attempts to find an inverse for the product of the A_is from first principles, that is, that we wish to determine B such that

$$(A_1 A_2 \cdots A_n) B = I$$

where B is the inverse matrix of the product. To remove A_1 from the product, we can then write

$$A_1^{-1} (A_1 A_2 \cdots A_n) B = A_1^{-1} I$$

which would reduce the equation to

$$(A_2 A_3 \cdots A_n) B = A_1^{-1} I.$$

Likewise, then, from

$$A_2^{-1}(A_2 A_3 \cdots A_n) B = A_2^{-1} A_1^{-1} I$$

which simplifies to

$$(\mathbf{A}_3\mathbf{A}_4\cdots\mathbf{A}_n)\mathbf{B} = \mathbf{A}_2^{-1}\mathbf{A}_1^{-1}\mathbf{I}.$$

If one repeat the process up to A_n, the equation becomes

$$\mathbf{B} = \mathbf{A}_n^{-1}\mathbf{A}_{n-1}^{-1}\cdots\mathbf{A}_2^{-1}\mathbf{A}_1^{-1}\mathbf{I}$$

$$\mathbf{B} = \mathbf{A}_n^{-1}\mathbf{A}_{n-1}^{-1}\cdots\mathbf{A}_2^{-1}\mathbf{A}_1^{-1}$$

but B is the inverse matrix, i.e. $\mathbf{B} = (\mathbf{A}_1\mathbf{A}_2\cdots\mathbf{A}_n)^{-1}$ so the property is established.

Over the field of real numbers, the set of singular n-by-n matrices, considered as a subset of $R^{n\times n}$, is a null set, i.e., has Lebesgue measure zero.

a. 2-bridge knot
b. Nonsingular
c. -equivalence
d. -module

16. In linear algebra, the _____ of a matrix A is another matrix A^T (also written A', A^{tr} or ^tA) created by any one of the following equivalent actions:

- write the rows of A as the columns of A^T
- write the columns of A as the rows of A^T
- reflect A by its main diagonal (which starts from the top left) to obtain A^T

Formally, the _____ of an m × n matrix A with elements A_{ij} is the n × m matrix

$$A^T_{ij} = A_{ji} \text{ for } 1 \leq i \leq n, 1 \leq j \leq m.$$

Chapter 3. DETERMINANTS

The _____ of a scalar is the same scalar.

- $\begin{bmatrix} 1 & 2 \end{bmatrix}^{\mathrm{T}} = \begin{bmatrix} 1 \\ 2 \end{bmatrix}.$

- $\begin{bmatrix} 1 & 2 \\ 3 & 4 \end{bmatrix}^{\mathrm{T}} = \begin{bmatrix} 1 & 3 \\ 2 & 4 \end{bmatrix}.$

- $\begin{bmatrix} 1 & 2 \\ 3 & 4 \\ 5 & 6 \end{bmatrix}^{\mathrm{T}} = \begin{bmatrix} 1 & 3 & 5 \\ 2 & 4 & 6 \end{bmatrix}.$

For matrices A, B and scalar c we have the following properties of _____:

1. $\left(\mathbf{A}^{\mathrm{T}}\right)^{\mathrm{T}} = \mathbf{A}$

   Taking the _____ is an involution (self inverse.)

- $(\mathbf{A} + \mathbf{B})^{\mathrm{T}} = \mathbf{A}^{\mathrm{T}} + \mathbf{B}^{\mathrm{T}}$

   The _____ respects addition.

- $(\mathbf{AB})^{\mathrm{T}} = \mathbf{B}^{\mathrm{T}} \mathbf{A}^{\mathrm{T}}$

   Note that the order of the factors reverses. From this one can deduce that a square matrix A is invertible if and only if A^T is invertible, and in this case we have $(A^{-1})^T = (A^T)^{-1}$. It is relatively easy to extend this result to the general case of multiple matrices, where we find that $(ABC...XYZ)^T = Z^T Y^T X^T ... C^T B^T A^T$.

- $(c\mathbf{A})^{\mathrm{T}} = c\mathbf{A}^{\mathrm{T}}$

   The _____ of a scalar is the same scalar. Together with (2), this states that the _____ is a linear map from the space of m × n matrices to the space of all n × m matrices.

- $\det(\mathbf{A}^{\mathrm{T}}) = \det(\mathbf{A})$

   The determinant of a square matrix is the same as that of its _____.

- The dot product of two column vectors a and b can be computed as

$$\mathbf{a} \cdot \mathbf{b} = \mathbf{a}^T \mathbf{b},$$

which is written as $a_i b^i$ in Einstein notation.

- If A has only real entries, then $A^T A$ is a positive-semidefinite matrix.
- $$(\mathbf{A}^T)^{-1} = (\mathbf{A}^{-1})^T$$

  The _____ of an invertible matrix is also invertible, and its inverse is the _____ of the inverse of the original matrix.

- If A is a square matrix, then its eigenvalues are equal to the eigenvalues of its _____.

A square matrix whose _____ is equal to itself is called a symmetric matrix; that is, A is symmetric if

$$\mathbf{A}^T = \mathbf{A}.$$

A square matrix whose _____ is also its inverse is called an orthogonal matrix; that is, G is orthogonal if

$$\mathbf{G}\mathbf{G}^T = \mathbf{G}^T\mathbf{G} = \mathbf{I}_n,$$ the identity matrix, i.e. $G^T = G^{-1}$.

A square matrix whose _____ is equal to its negative is called skew-symmetric matrix; that is, A is skew-symmetric if

$$\mathbf{A}^T = -\mathbf{A}.$$

The conjugate _____ of the complex matrix A, written as A^*, is obtained by taking the _____ of A and the complex conjugate of each entry:

$$\mathbf{A}^* = (\overline{\mathbf{A}})^T = \overline{(\mathbf{A}^T)}.$$

If f: V→W is a linear map between vector spaces V and W with nondegenerate bilinear forms, we define the _____ of f to be the linear map ${}^t f$: W→V, determined by

$$B_V(v, {}^t f(w)) = B_W(f(v), w) \quad \forall \ v \in V, w \in W.$$

Here, B_V and B_W are the bilinear forms on V and W respectively. The matrix of the _____ of a map is the transposed matrix only if the bases are orthonormal with respect to their bilinear forms.

Over a complex vector space, one often works with sesquilinear forms instead of bilinear (conjugate-linear in one argument.)

Chapter 3. DETERMINANTS

a. Transpose
b. Drazin inverse
c. Levinson recursion
d. Tridiagonal matrix

17. In mathematics, two vectors are _____ if they are perpendicular, i.e., they form a right angle. The word comes from the Greek á½€ρθÏŒς , meaning 'straight', and γωνῖα (gonia), meaning 'angle'. For example, a subway and the street above, although they do not physically intersect, are _____ if they cross at a right angle.
   a. Embedding
   b. Orthogonal
   c. Unital
   d. Expression

18. In linear algebra, an _____ is a square matrix with real entries whose columns (or rows) are orthogonal unit vectors (i.e., orthonormal.) Equivalently, a matrix Q is orthogonal if its transpose is equal to its inverse:

$$Q^T Q = QQ^T = I.$$

As a linear transformation, an _____ preserves the dot product of vectors, and therefore acts as an isometry of Euclidean space, such as a rotation or reflection.

The set of n × n orthogonal matrices forms a group O(n), known as the orthogonal group.

   a. Unistochastic matrix
   b. Alternating sign matrix
   c. Orthogonal matrix
   d. Unimodular matrix

19. For each eigenvector of a linear transformation, there is a corresponding scalar value called an _____ for that vector, which determines the amount the eigenvector is scaled under the linear transformation. For example, an _____ of +2 means that the eigenvector is doubled in length and points in the same direction. An _____ of +1 means that the eigenvector is unchanged, while an _____ of −1 means that the eigenvector is reversed in sense.
   a. ADE classification
   b. AKS primality test
   c. Abelian P-root group
   d. Eigenvalue

Chapter 3. DETERMINANTS

20. For each _____ of a linear transformation, there is a corresponding scalar value called an eigenvalue for that vector, which determines the amount the _____ is scaled under the linear transformation. For example, an eigenvalue of +2 means that the _____ is doubled in length and points in the same direction. An eigenvalue of +1 means that the _____ is unchanged, while an eigenvalue of −1 means that the _____ is reversed in sense.

   a. AKS primality test
   b. Abelian P-root group
   c. Eigenvector
   d. ADE classification

21. In mathematics, the _____ of a ring R, often denoted char(R), is defined to be the smallest number of times one must add the ring's multiplicative identity element (1) to itself to get the additive identity element (0); the ring is said to have _____ zero if this repeated sum never reaches the additive identity. That is, char(R) is the smallest positive number n such that

$$\underbrace{1 + \cdots + 1}_{n \text{ summands}} = 0$$

if such a number n exists, and 0 otherwise. The _____ may also be taken to be the exponent of the ring's additive group, that is, the smallest positive n such that

$$\underbrace{a + \cdots + a}_{n \text{ summands}} = 0$$

for every element a of the ring (again, if n exists; otherwise zero.)

   a. Characteristic
   b. Coherent ring
   c. Free ideal ring
   d. Hereditary

22. In discrete mathematics, the _____ is used when solving recurrence problems. One can specify a recurrence relation of the form

$$t_n = At_{n-1} + Bt_{n-2}$$

where the value of t_n is dependent on the values of t_{n-1} and t_{n-2}. When solving a recurrence relation, the goal is to eliminate this dependency and derive an equation of the form

$$t_n = c_1 r_1^n + c_2 r_2^n,$$

Chapter 3. DETERMINANTS

where c_1 and c_2 are constants and r_1 and r_2 are the roots of the _____

$$r^2 - Ar - B = 0,$$

where A and B are the constants defined in the original recurrence relation.

   a. 2-bridge knot
   b. -module
   c. Characteristic equation
   d. -equivalence

23. A _____ is one of the basic shapes of geometry: a polygon with three corners or vertices and three sides or edges which are line segments. A _____ with vertices A, B, and C is denoted ABC.

In Euclidean geometry any three non-collinear points determine a unique _____ and a unique plane (i.e. a two-dimensional Euclidean space.)

   a. 2-bridge knot
   b. Triangle
   c. -module
   d. -equivalence

24. In geometry, a _____ is a straight curve. When geometry is used to model the real world, lines are used to represent straight objects with negligible width and height. Lines are an idealisation of such objects and have no width or height at all and are usually considered to be infinitely long.
   a. -module
   b. 2-bridge knot
   c. -equivalence
   d. Line

25. In mathematics, a _____ is a flat surface. Planes can arise as subspaces of some higher dimensional space, as with the walls of a room, or they may enjoy an independent existence in their own right, as in the setting of Euclidean geometry

Chapter 3. DETERMINANTS

a. Plane
b. -module
c. -equivalence
d. Similarity

26. _____ is the mathematical process of putting things together. The plus sign '+' means that numbers are added together. For example, in the picture on the right, there are 3 + 2 apples--meaning three apples and two other apples--which is the same as five apples, since 3 + 2 = 5.

   a. Abelian P-root group
   b. ADE classification
   c. AKS primality test
   d. Addition

27. In mathematics the _____ of a set which is equipped with the operation of addition is an element which, when added to any element x in the set, yields x. One of the most familiar additive identities is the number 0 from elementary mathematics, but additive identities occur in other mathematical structures where addition is defined, such as in groups and rings.

- The _____ familiar from elementary mathematics is zero, denoted 0. For example,

    5 + 0 = 5 = 0 + 5.

- In the natural numbers N and all of its supersets (the integers Z, the rational numbers Q, the real numbers R, or the complex numbers C), the _____ is 0. Thus for any one of these numbers n,

    n + 0 = n = 0 + n.

Let N be a set which is closed under the operation of addition, denoted +. An _____ for N is any element e such that for any element n in N,

   e + n = n = n + e.

   a. Identity element
   b. External
   c. Universal algebra
   d. Additive identity

28. In mathematics, the _____ of a number n is the number that, when added to n, yields zero. The _____ of F is denoted −F.

Chapter 3. DETERMINANTS 35

For example, the _____ of 7 is −7, because 7 + (−7) = 0, and the _____ of −0.3 is 0.3, because −0.3 + 0.3 = 0.

a. Artinian ideal
b. Interior algebra
c. Isomorphism class
d. Additive inverse

29. In mathematics, _____ is one of the basic operations defining a vector space in linear algebra Note that _____ is different from scalar product which is an inner product between two vectors.

More specifically, if K is a field and V is a vector space over K, then _____ is a function from K × V to V. The result of applying this function to c in K and v in V is denoted cv.

a. Matrix pencil
b. K-frame
c. Symplectic vector space
d. Scalar multiplication

30. In abstract algebra, an _____ is a bijective map f such that both f and its inverse f^{-1} are homomorphisms, i.e., structure-preserving mappings. In the more general setting of category theory, an _____ is a morphism f:X→Y in a category for which there exists an 'inverse' f^{-1}:Y→X, with the property that both $f^{-1}f=id_X$ and $ff^{-1}=id_Y$.

Informally, an _____ is a kind of mapping between objects, which shows a relationship between two properties or operations.

a. Isomorphism
b. Endomorphism
c. ADE classification
d. Epimorphism

31. In vector calculus, the _____ is shorthand for either the _____ matrix or its determinant, the _____ determinant.

In algebraic geometry the _____ of a curve means the _____ variety: a group variety associated to the curve, in which the curve can be embedded.

These concepts are all named after the mathematician Carl Gustav Jacob Jacobi.

a. Jacobian
b. Laplace operator
c. Hessian matrix
d. Critical point

32. In linear algebra, one associates a polynomial to every square matrix, its _____. This polynomial encodes several important properties of the matrix, most notably its eigenvalues, its determinant and its trace.

Given a square matrix A, we want to find a polynomial whose roots are precisely the eigenvalues of A. For a diagonal matrix A, the _____ is easy to define: if the diagonal entries are a_1, a_2, a_3, etc.

a. Quasi-polynomial
b. Square-free polynomial
c. Constant term
d. Characteristic polynomial

Chapter 4. VECTOR SPACES

1. In mathematics, in the field of group theory, a _____ of a finite group is a quasisimple subnormal subgroup. Any two distinct components commute. The product of all the components is the layer of the group.
    a. Stallings' theorem about ends of groups
    b. Wreath product
    c. Group homomorphism
    d. Component

2. _____ is the mathematical process of putting things together. The plus sign '+' means that numbers are added together. For example, in the picture on the right, there are 3 + 2 apples--meaning three apples and two other apples--which is the same as five apples, since 3 + 2 = 5.
    a. ADE classification
    b. Abelian P-root group
    c. AKS primality test
    d. Addition

3. In geometry, a _____ is a straight curve. When geometry is used to model the real world, lines are used to represent straight objects with negligible width and height. Lines are an idealisation of such objects and have no width or height at all and are usually considered to be infinitely long.
    a. -module
    b. 2-bridge knot
    c. -equivalence
    d. Line

4. In geometry, a _____ is a part of a line that is bounded by two end points, and contains every point on the line between its end points. Examples of line segments include the sides of a triangle or square. More generally, when the end points are both vertices of a polygon, the _____ is either an edge (of that polygon) if they are adjacent vertices, or otherwise a diagonal.
    a. -module
    b. -equivalence
    c. Skew lines
    d. Line segment

5. In mathematics, a (B, N) _____ is a structure on groups of Lie type that allows one to give uniform proofs of many results, instead of giving a large number of case-by-case proofs. Roughly speaking, it shows that all such groups are similar to the general linear group over a field. They were invented by the mathematician Jacques Tits, and are also sometimes known as Tits systems.

Chapter 4. VECTOR SPACES

a. Group representations
b. Rank of a group
c. Group action
d. Pair

6. In mathematics, a _____ is a flat surface. Planes can arise as subspaces of some higher dimensional space, as with the walls of a room, or they may enjoy an independent existence in their own right, as in the setting of Euclidean geometry

a. -equivalence
b. -module
c. Similarity
d. Plane

7. The column _____ of a matrix A is the maximal number of linearly independent columns of A. Likewise, the row _____ is the maximal number of linearly independent rows of A.

Since the column _____ and the row _____ are always equal, they are simply called the _____ of A. More abstractly, it is the dimension of the image of A. For the proofs, see, e.g., Murase (1960), Andrea ' Wong (1960), Williams ' Cater (1968), Mackiw (1995.) It is commonly denoted by either rk(A) or _____ A.

a. Generalized Pauli matrices
b. Schur complement
c. Rank
d. Split-complex number

8. The real component of a quaternion is also called its _____ part.

The term is also sometimes used informally to mean a vector, matrix, tensor, or other usually 'compound' value that is actually reduced to a single component. Thus, for example, the product of a 1×n matrix and an n×1 matrix, which is formally a 1×1 matrix, is often said to be a _____.

a. Self-adjoint
b. Tensor product
c. Distributivity
d. Scalar

Chapter 4. VECTOR SPACES

9. In mathematics, _____ is one of the basic operations defining a vector space in linear algebra Note that _____ is different from scalar product which is an inner product between two vectors.

More specifically, if K is a field and V is a vector space over K, then _____ is a function from K × V to V. The result of applying this function to c in K and v in V is denoted cv.

   a. Matrix pencil
   b. Symplectic vector space
   c. Scalar multiplication
   d. K-frame

10. _____ is one of the four basic arithmetic operations; it is the inverse of addition, meaning that if we start with any number and add any number and then subtract the same number we added, we return to the number we started with. _____ is denoted by a minus sign in infix notation.

The traditional names for the parts of the formula

   c − b = a

are minuend (c) − subtrahend (b) = difference (a.)

   a. -module
   b. 2-bridge knot
   c. -equivalence
   d. Subtraction

11. In mathematics the _____ of a set which is equipped with the operation of addition is an element which, when added to any element x in the set, yields x. One of the most familiar additive identities is the number 0 from elementary mathematics, but additive identities occur in other mathematical structures where addition is defined, such as in groups and rings.

- The _____ familiar from elementary mathematics is zero, denoted 0. For example,

   $5 + 0 = 5 = 0 + 5.$

- In the natural numbers N and all of its supersets (the integers Z, the rational numbers Q, the real numbers R, or the complex numbers C), the _____ is 0. Thus for any one of these numbers n,

   $n + 0 = n = 0 + n.$

Let N be a set which is closed under the operation of addition, denoted +. An _____ for N is any element e such that for any element n in N,

e + n = n = n + e.

a. Additive identity
b. Identity element
c. Universal algebra
d. External

12. In mathematics, the _____ of a number n is the number that, when added to n, yields zero. The _____ of F is denoted −F.

For example, the _____ of 7 is −7, because 7 + (−7) = 0, and the _____ of −0.3 is 0.3, because −0.3 + 0.3 = 0.

a. Artinian ideal
b. Additive inverse
c. Isomorphism class
d. Interior algebra

13. In mathematics, a _____ is a rectangular array of numbers. This way, matrices can record data that depend on multiple parameters. In particular they are used to keep track of the coefficients of multiple linear equations. Matrices are closely connected to linear transformations, which are higher-dimensional analogs of linear functions, i.e., functions of the form f(x) = c Â· x, where c is a constant. This map corresponds to a _____ with one row and column, with entry c. In addition to a number of elementary, entrywise operations such as _____ addition a key notion is _____ multiplication, which displays a number of features not encountered in numbers; for example, products of matrices depend on the order of the factors, unlike products of real numbers, say, where c Â· d = d Â· c for any two numbers c and d.
a. Heap
b. Polynomial expression
c. Matrix
d. Commutativity

14. In mathematics, _____ is the operation of adding two matrices by adding the corresponding entries together. However, there is another operation which could also be considered as a kind of addition for matrices.

The usual _____ is defined for two matrices of the same dimensions.

Chapter 4. VECTOR SPACES

a. Projection-valued measure
b. Cofactor
c. Nonlinear eigenproblem
d. Matrix addition

15. In its simplest meaning in mathematics and logic, an _____ is an action or procedure which produces a new value from one or more input values. There are two common types of operations: unary and binary. Unary operations involve only one value, such as negation and trigonometric functions.
    a. AKS primality test
    b. ADE classification
    c. Abelian P-root group
    d. Operation

16. In abstract algebra, the _____ is a construction which combines several modules into a new, larger module. The result of the direct summation of modules is the 'smallest general' module which contains the given modules as subspaces. This is an example of a coproduct.
    a. Schmidt decomposition
    b. Finite dimensional von Neumann algebra
    c. Frame
    d. Direct sum

17. In mathematics, the _____ of two sets A and B is the set that contains all elements of A that also belong to B (or equivalently, all elements of B that also belong to A), but no other elements.

For explanation of the symbols used in this article, refer to the table of mathematical symbols.

The _____ of A and B

The _____ of A and B is written 'A ∩ B'.

    a. AKS primality test
    b. Abelian P-root group
    c. ADE classification
    d. Intersection

18. In mathematics, _____ are a concept central to linear algebra and related fields of mathematics

Chapter 4. VECTOR SPACES

Suppose that K is a field and V is a vector space over K. As usual, we call elements of V vectors and call elements of K scalars.

a. Left alternative
b. Groupoid
c. Hyperstructures
d. Linear combinations

19. In linear algebra, a family of vectors is _____ if none of them can be written as a linear combination of finitely many other vectors in the collection. A family of vectors which is not _____ is called linearly dependent. For instance, in the three-dimensional real vector space $\mathbb{R}^3$ we have the following example.

a. Composition ring
b. Grothendieck group
c. Linearly independent
d. Derivative algebra

20. Let S be a set with a binary operation * . If e is an identity element of (S, *) and a * b = e, then a is called a _____ of b and b is called a right inverse of a. If an element x is both a _____ and a right inverse of y, then x is called a two-sided inverse, or simply an inverse, of y.

a. -module
b. Left inverse
c. 2-bridge knot
d. -equivalence

21. In linear algebra, a _____ is a set of vectors that, in a linear combination, can represent every vector in a given vector space or free module, and such that no element of the set can be represented as a linear combination of the others. In other words, a _____ is a linearly independent spanning set.

a. Supergroup
b. Chirality
c. Basis
d. Minor

22. In mathematics, the _____ for a Euclidean space consists of one unit vector pointing in the direction of each axis of the Cartesian coordinate system. For example, the _____ for the Euclidean plane are the vectors

Chapter 4. VECTOR SPACES

$$\mathbf{e}_x = (1,0), \quad \mathbf{e}_y = (0,1),$$

and the _____ for three-dimensional space are the vectors

$$\mathbf{e}_x = (1,0,0), \quad \mathbf{e}_y = (0,1,0), \quad \mathbf{e}_z = (0,0,1).$$

Here the vector e_x points in the x direction, the vector e_y points in the y direction, and the vector e_z points in the z direction. There are several common notations for these vectors, including {e_x, e_y, e_z}, {e_1, e_2, e_3}, {i, j, k}, and {x, y, z}.

   a. Standard basis
   b. -equivalence
   c. -module
   d. 2-bridge knot

23. In mathematics, the _____ of a vector space V is the cardinality (i.e. the number of vectors) of a basis of V. It is sometimes called Hamel _____ or algebraic _____ to distinguish it from other types of _____. All bases of a vector space have equal cardinality and so the _____ of a vector space is uniquely defined. The _____ of the vector space V over the field F can be written as $\dim_F(V)$ or as [V : F], read '_____ of V over F'.

   a. Cofactor
   b. Dual basis
   c. Partial trace
   d. Dimension

24. In linear algebra, the _____ of a matrix A is the collection of cells $A_{i,j}$ where i is equal to j.

The _____ of a square matrix is the diagonal which runs from the top left corner to the bottom right corner. For example, the following matrix has 1s down its _____:

$$\begin{bmatrix} 1 & 0 & 0 \\ 0 & 1 & 0 \\ 0 & 0 & 1 \end{bmatrix}.$$

A square matrix like the above in which the entries outside the _____ are all zero is called a diagonal matrix.

Chapter 4. VECTOR SPACES

a. Diagonalizable matrix
b. Complex Hadamard matrix
c. Polynomial matrix
d. Main diagonal

25. The _____ of an m-by-n matrix with real entries is the subspace of R^n generated by the row vectors of the matrix. Its dimension is equal to the rank of the matrix and is at most min(m,n.)

The column space of an m-by-n matrix with real entries is the subspace of R^m generated by the column vectors of the matrix.

a. Restriction of scalars
b. Goodman-Nguyen-van Fraassen algebra
c. Differential graded algebra
d. Row space

26. In linear algebra, the _____ of a matrix is the set of all possible linear combinations of its column vectors. The _____ of an m × n matrix is a subspace of m-dimensional Euclidean space. The dimension of the _____ is called the rank of the matrix.

a. Pseudovector
b. Column space
c. Delta operator
d. Linear inequality

27. A _____ is a mathematical equation for an unknown function of one or several variables that relates the values of the function itself and its derivatives of various orders. Differential equations play a prominent role in engineering, physics, economics and other disciplines. Visualization of airflow into a duct modelled using the Navier-Stokes equations, a set of partial differential equations.

Differential equations arise in many areas of science and technology; whenever a deterministic relationship involving some continuously changing quantities (modeled by functions) and their rates of change (expressed as derivatives) is known or postulated.

a. -module
b. 2-bridge knot
c. Differential equation
d. -equivalence

Chapter 4. VECTOR SPACES

28. In mathematics, a _____ is a collection of linear equations involving the same set of variables. For example,

$$3x + 2y - z = 1$$
$$2x - 2y + 4z = -2$$
$$-x + \tfrac{1}{2}y - z = 0$$

is a system of three equations in the three variables x, y, z. A solution to a linear system is an assignment of numbers to the variables such that all the equations are simultaneously satisfied.

   a. System of linear equations
   b. -equivalence
   c. -module
   d. Simultaneous equations

29. In linear algebra, two vectors in an inner product space are _____ if they are orthogonal and both of unit length. A set of vectors form an _____ set if all vectors in the set are mutually orthogonal and all of unit length. An _____ set which forms a basis is called an _____ basis.
   a. Elementary matrix
   b. Invertible matrix
   c. Orthonormal
   d. Overdetermined

30. In mathematics, an _____ of an inner product space V (i.e., a vector space with an inner product), is a set of mutually orthogonal vectors of magnitude 1 (unit vectors) that span the space when infinite linear combinations are allowed. (In some contexts, especially in linear algebra, the concept of basis (linear algebra) means a set of vectors that span a space when only finite linear combinations are allowed.) Such an infinite linear combination is an infinite series, and the concept of convergence relied upon is defined in terms of the space's inner product.
   a. Orthonormal basis
   b. Orientation
   c. Overdetermined
   d. Eigendecomposition

31. In linear algebra, a basis for a vector space of dimension n is a sequence of n vectors $\alpha_1, ..., \alpha_n$ with the property that every vector in the space can be expressed uniquely as a linear combination of the basis vectors. Since it is often desirable to work with more than one basis for a vector space, it is of fundamental importance in linear algebra to be able to easily transform coordinate-wise representations of vectors and linear transformations taken with respect to one basis to their equivalent representations with respect to another basis. Such a transformation is called a _____.

Chapter 4. VECTOR SPACES

a. Split-complex number
b. Change of basis
c. Generalized singular value decomposition
d. Field of values

32. In mathematics, a _____ is a function between two vector spaces that preserves the operations of vector addition and scalar multiplication. The expression 'linear operator' is in especially common use, for linear maps from a vector space to itself In advanced mathematics, the definition of linear function coincides with the definition of _____.

a. Real matrices
b. Rotation
c. Homomorphic secret sharing
d. Linear map

33. In mathematics, an _____ is the finite or bounded case of a conic section, the geometric shape that results from cutting a circular conical or cylindrical surface with an oblique plane . It is also the locus of all points of the plane whose distances to two fixed points add to the same constant.

Ellipses also arise as images of a circle or a sphere under parallel projection, and some cases of perspective projection.

a. Ellipse
b. AKS primality test
c. Abelian P-root group
d. ADE classification

34. In mathematics, the _____ is a conic section, the intersection of a right circular conical surface and a plane parallel to a generating straight line of that surface. Given a point (the focus) and a line (the directrix) that lie in a plane, the locus of points in that plane that are equidistant to them is a _____.

A particular case arises when the plane is tangent to the conical surface of a circle.

a. -module
b. 2-bridge knot
c. Parabola
d. -equivalence

35. In geometry and linear algebra, a _____ is a transformation in a plane or in space that describes the motion of a rigid body around a fixed point. A _____ is different from a translation, which has no fixed points, and from a reflection, which 'flips' the bodies it is transforming. A _____ and the above-mentioned transformations are isometries; they leave the distance between any two points unchanged after the transformation.
   a. Rotation
   b. Real matrices
   c. Reflection
   d. Shear mappings

Chapter 5. INNER PRODUCT SPACES

1. In abstract algebra, the _____ of a module is a measure of the module's 'size'. It is defined as the _____ of the longest ascending chain of submodules and is a generalization of the concept of dimension for vector spaces. The modules with finite _____ share many important properties with finite-dimensional vector spaces.

   a. Finitely generated module
   b. Supermodule
   c. Morita equivalence
   d. Length

2. In mathematics, in the field of group theory, a _____ of a finite group is a quasisimple subnormal subgroup. Any two distinct components commute. The product of all the components is the layer of the group.

   a. Wreath product
   b. Group homomorphism
   c. Stallings' theorem about ends of groups
   d. Component

3. In linear algebra, functional analysis and related areas of mathematics, a _____ is a function that assigns a strictly positive length or size to all vectors in a vector space, other than the zero vector. A seminorm (or pseudonorm), on the other hand, is allowed to assign zero length to some non-zero vectors.

   A simple example is the 2-dimensional Euclidean space R^2 equipped with the Euclidean _____.

   a. Quasinorm
   b. -module
   c. -equivalence
   d. Norm

4. In mathematics, a _____ in a (unital) ring R is an invertible element of R, i.e. an element u such that there is a v in R with

   $uv = vu = 1_R$, where 1_R is the multiplicative identity element.

   That is, u is an invertible element of the multiplicative monoid of R. If $0 \neq 1$ in the ring, then 0 is not a _____.

   Unfortunately, the term _____ is also used to refer to the identity element 1_R of the ring, in expressions like ring with a _____ or _____ ring, and also e.g. '_____' matrix.

Chapter 5. INNER PRODUCT SPACES

a. Ore extension
b. Unit
c. Ore condition
d. Ascending chain condition on principal ideals

5. The real component of a quaternion is also called its _____ part.

The term is also sometimes used informally to mean a vector, matrix, tensor, or other usually 'compound' value that is actually reduced to a single component. Thus, for example, the product of a 1×n matrix and an n×1 matrix, which is formally a 1×1 matrix, is often said to be a _____.

a. Distributivity
b. Scalar
c. Tensor product
d. Self-adjoint

6. In mathematics, _____ is one of the basic operations defining a vector space in linear algebra Note that _____ is different from scalar product which is an inner product between two vectors.

More specifically, if K is a field and V is a vector space over K, then _____ is a function from K × V to V. The result of applying this function to c in K and v in V is denoted cv.

a. K-frame
b. Symplectic vector space
c. Scalar multiplication
d. Matrix pencil

7. In mathematics, a _____ is a quadric, a type of surface in three dimensions, described by the equation

$$\frac{x^2}{a^2} + \frac{y^2}{b^2} - \frac{z^2}{c^2} = 1$$

_____ of one sheet,

or

$$-\frac{x^2}{a^2} - \frac{y^2}{b^2} + \frac{z^2}{c^2} = 1$$

_____ of two sheets.

These are also called elliptical hyperboloids. If, and only if, a = b, it is a _____ of revolution, and is also called a circular _____.

a. 2-bridge knot
b. -equivalence
c. Hyperboloid
d. -module

8. In mathematics, the _____ of a number n is the number that, when added to n, yields zero. The _____ of F is denoted −F.

For example, the _____ of 7 is −7, because 7 + (−7) = 0, and the _____ of −0.3 is 0.3, because −0.3 + 0.3 = 0.

a. Interior algebra
b. Isomorphism class
c. Artinian ideal
d. Additive inverse

9. In mathematics, the _____ is an operation which takes two vectors over the real numbers R and returns a real-valued scalar quantity. It is the standard inner product of the orthonormal Euclidean space. It contrasts with the cross product which produces a vector result.

a. Centrosymmetric matrix
b. Coefficient matrix
c. Complex structure
d. Dot product

10. In mathematics, an _____ is a statement about the relative size or order of two objects, or about whether they are the same or not

- The notation a < b means that a is less than b.
- The notation a > b means that a is greater than b.
- The notation a ≠ b means that a is not equal to b, but does not say that one is bigger than the other or even that they can be compared in size.

In all these cases, a is not equal to b, hence, '_____'.

These relations are known as strict _____

- The notation a ≤ b means that a is less than or equal to b (or, equivalently, not greater than b);
- The notation a ≥ b means that a is greater than or equal to b (or, equivalently, not smaller than b);

An additional use of the notation is to show that one quantity is much greater than another, normally by several orders of magnitude.

- The notation a ≪ b means that a is much less than b.
- The notation a ≫ b means that a is much greater than b.

If the sense of the _____ is the same for all values of the variables for which its members are defined, then the _____ is called an 'absolute' or 'unconditional' _____. If the sense of an _____ holds only for certain values of the variables involved, but is reversed or destroyed for other values of the variables, it is called a conditional _____.

One can apply the same algebraic operations to inequalities as one would apply for solving equalities. For example, to find x for the _____ 10x > 20 one would divide 20 by 10 to obtain x > 2.

   a. ADE classification
   b. Abelian P-root group
   c. Inequality
   d. AKS primality test

11.   In geometry and trigonometry, an _____ is the figure formed by two rays sharing a common endpoint, called the vertex of the _____ . The magnitude of the _____ is the 'amount of rotation' that separates the two rays, and can be measured by considering the length of circular arc swept out when one ray is rotated about the vertex to coincide with the other Where there is no possibility of confusion, the term '_____' is used interchangeably for both the geometric configuration itself and for its angular magnitude (which is simply a numerical quantity.)
   a. Abelian P-root group
   b. ADE classification
   c. AKS primality test
   d. Angle

12.   In mathematics, two vectors are _____ if they are perpendicular, i.e., they form a right angle. The word comes from the Greek ὀρθίος , meaning 'straight', and γωνία (gonia), meaning 'angle'. For example, a subway and the street above, although they do not physically intersect, are _____ if they cross at a right angle.

a. Embedding
b. Unital
c. Orthogonal
d. Expression

13. A _____ is one of the basic shapes of geometry: a polygon with three corners or vertices and three sides or edges which are line segments. A _____ with vertices A, B, and C is denoted ABC.

In Euclidean geometry any three non-collinear points determine a unique _____ and a unique plane (i.e. a two-dimensional Euclidean space.)

a. -equivalence
b. -module
c. Triangle
d. 2-bridge knot

14. In mathematics, the _____ states that for any triangle, the length of a given side must be less than the sum of the other two sides but greater than the difference between the two sides.

In Euclidean geometry and some other geometries this is a theorem. In the Euclidean case, in both the less than or equal to and greater than or equal to statements, equality occurs only if the triangle has a 180° angle and two 0° angles, as shown in the bottom example in the image to the right.

a. 2-bridge knot
b. -equivalence
c. -module
d. Triangle Inequality

15. The a-_____ of a string, for a a letter, is the number of times that letter occurs in the string. More precisely, let A be a finite set (called the alphabet), $a \in A$ a letter of A, and $c \in A^*$ a string (where A* is the free monoid generated by the elements of A, equivalently the set of strings, including the empty string, whose letters are from A.) Then the a-_____ of c, denoted by $wt_a(c)$, is the number of times the generator a occurs in the unique expression for c as a product (concatenation) of letters in A.

a. Presentation of a monoid
b. Weight
c. Biordered set
d. Trace monoid

Chapter 5. INNER PRODUCT SPACES

16. In mathematics the _____ of a set which is equipped with the operation of addition is an element which, when added to any element x in the set, yields x. One of the most familiar additive identities is the number 0 from elementary mathematics, but additive identities occur in other mathematical structures where addition is defined, such as in groups and rings.

- The _____ familiar from elementary mathematics is zero, denoted 0. For example,

5 + 0 = 5 = 0 + 5.

- In the natural numbers N and all of its supersets (the integers Z, the rational numbers Q, the real numbers R, or the complex numbers C), the _____ is 0. Thus for any one of these numbers n,

n + 0 = n = 0 + n.

Let N be a set which is closed under the operation of addition, denoted +. An _____ for N is any element e such that for any element n in N,

e + n = n = n + e.

a. Additive identity
b. External
c. Universal algebra
d. Identity element

17. In linear algebra and functional analysis, a _____ is a linear transformation P from a vector space to itself such that $P^2 = P$. It leaves its image unchanged. Though abstract, this definition of '_____' formalizes and generalizes the idea of graphical _____.
a. C_0-semigroup
b. Projection
c. Convolution power
d. Lumer-Phillips theorem

18. In linear algebra, a _____ is a set of vectors that, in a linear combination, can represent every vector in a given vector space or free module, and such that no element of the set can be represented as a linear combination of the others. In other words, a _____ is a linearly independent spanning set.
a. Chirality
b. Minor
c. Basis
d. Supergroup

Chapter 5. INNER PRODUCT SPACES

19. In linear algebra, two vectors in an inner product space are _____ if they are orthogonal and both of unit length. A set of vectors form an _____ set if all vectors in the set are mutually orthogonal and all of unit length. An _____ set which forms a basis is called an _____ basis.
    a. Orthonormal
    b. Overdetermined
    c. Elementary matrix
    d. Invertible matrix

20. In mathematics, an _____ of an inner product space V (i.e., a vector space with an inner product), is a set of mutually orthogonal vectors of magnitude 1 (unit vectors) that span the space when infinite linear combinations are allowed. (In some contexts, especially in linear algebra, the concept of basis (linear algebra) means a set of vectors that span a space when only finite linear combinations are allowed.) Such an infinite linear combination is an infinite series, and the concept of convergence relied upon is defined in terms of the space's inner product.
    a. Eigendecomposition
    b. Orientation
    c. Orthonormal Basis
    d. Overdetermined

21. In linear algebra, a family of vectors is _____ if none of them can be written as a linear combination of finitely many other vectors in the collection. A family of vectors which is not _____ is called linearly dependent. For instance, in the three-dimensional real vector space $\mathbb{R}^3$ we have the following example.
    a. Composition ring
    b. Derivative algebra
    c. Grothendieck group
    d. Linearly independent

22. In mathematics, a _____ is a constant multiplicative factor of a certain object. For example, in the expression $9x^2$, the _____ of x^2 is 9.

The object can be such things as a variable, a vector, a function, etc.

    a. Coefficient
    b. Tschirnhaus transformation
    c. Vandermonde polynomial
    d. Constant term

23. These solutions for n = 0, 1, 2, ... (with the normalization $P_n(1) = 1$) form a polynomial sequence of orthogonal polynomials called the Legendre polynomials. Each _____ $P_n(x)$ is an nth-degree polynomial.

Chapter 5. INNER PRODUCT SPACES

a. Legendre polynomial
b. -equivalence
c. Jacobi polynomial
d. -module

24. The method of _____ is used to approximately solve overdetermined systems, i.e. systems of equations in which there are more equations than unknowns. _____ is often applied in statistical contexts, particularly regression analysis.

_____ can be interpreted as a method of fitting data.

a. -module
b. 2-bridge knot
c. -equivalence
d. Least squares

25. In geometry, a _____ is a straight curve. When geometry is used to model the real world, lines are used to represent straight objects with negligible width and height. Lines are an idealisation of such objects and have no width or height at all and are usually considered to be infinitely long.

a. -equivalence
b. -module
c. 2-bridge knot
d. Line

26. In the mathematical fields of linear algebra and functional analysis, the _____ $W^\perp$ of a subspace W of an inner product space V is the set of all vectors in V that are orthogonal to every vector in W, i.e., it is

$$W^\perp = \{x \in V : \langle x, y \rangle = 0 \text{ for all } y \in W\}.$$

Informally, it is called the perp, short for perpendicular complement.

The _____ is always closed in the metric topology. In finite-dimensional spaces, that is merely an instance of the fact that all subspaces of a vector space are closed.

a. Independent equation
b. Invariant subspace
c. Orthogonal complement
d. Euclidean subspace

Chapter 5. INNER PRODUCT SPACES

27. Definition. Two vector subspaces A and B of an inner product space V are called _____ if each vector in A is orthogonal to each vector in B. The largest subspace that is orthogonal to a given subspace is its orthogonal complement.
   a. AKS primality test
   b. ADE classification
   c. Orthogonal subspaces
   d. Abelian P-root group

28. In discrete mathematics and predominantly in set theory, a _____ is a concept used in comparisons of sets to refer to the unique values of one set in relation to another. The terms 'absolute' and 'relative' _____ refer to more specific applications of the concept, with universal complements referring to elements unique to the universal set and the latter referring to the unique elements of one set in relation to another. In this image, the universal set is represented by the border of the image, and the set A as a disc.
   a. -module
   b. Pointed set
   c. -equivalence
   d. Complement

29. In abstract algebra, the _____ is a construction which combines several modules into a new, larger module. The result of the direct summation of modules is the 'smallest general' module which contains the given modules as subspaces. This is an example of a coproduct.
   a. Finite dimensional von Neumann algebra
   b. Direct sum
   c. Frame
   d. Schmidt decomposition

30. In mathematics, a _____ is a rectangular array of numbers. This way, matrices can record data that depend on multiple parameters. In particular they are used to keep track of the coefficients of multiple linear equations. Matrices are closely connected to linear transformations, which are higher-dimensional analogs of linear functions, i.e., functions of the form f(x) = c Â· x, where c is a constant. This map corresponds to a _____ with one row and column, with entry c. In addition to a number of elementary, entrywise operations such as _____ addition a key notion is _____ multiplication, which displays a number of features not encountered in numbers; for example, products of matrices depend on the order of the factors, unlike products of real numbers, say, where c Â· d = d Â· c for any two numbers c and d.
   a. Heap
   b. Polynomial expression
   c. Matrix
   d. Commutativity

Chapter 5. INNER PRODUCT SPACES

31. In mathematics, the _____ is a binary operation on two vectors in a three-dimensional Euclidean space that results in another vector which is perpendicular to the plane containing the two input vectors. The algebra defined by the _____ is neither commutative nor associative. It contrasts with the dot product which produces a scalar result.

   a. Differential graded algebra
   b. Row space
   c. Formal power series
   d. Cross product

32. In linear algebra, an _____ is a square matrix with real entries whose columns (or rows) are orthogonal unit vectors (i.e., orthonormal.) Equivalently, a matrix Q is orthogonal if its transpose is equal to its inverse:

$$Q^T Q = QQ^T = I.$$

As a linear transformation, an _____ preserves the dot product of vectors, and therefore acts as an isometry of Euclidean space, such as a rotation or reflection.

The set of n × n orthogonal matrices forms a group O(n), known as the orthogonal group.

   a. Unistochastic matrix
   b. Alternating sign matrix
   c. Unimodular matrix
   d. Orthogonal matrix

33. In linear algebra, the _____ of a matrix A is the collection of cells $A_{i,j}$ where i is equal to j.

The _____ of a square matrix is the diagonal which runs from the top left corner to the bottom right corner. For example, the following matrix has 1s down its _____:

$$\begin{bmatrix} 1 & 0 & 0 \\ 0 & 1 & 0 \\ 0 & 0 & 1 \end{bmatrix}.$$

A square matrix like the above in which the entries outside the _____ are all zero is called a diagonal matrix.

   a. Diagonalizable matrix
   b. Polynomial matrix
   c. Complex Hadamard matrix
   d. Main diagonal

Chapter 6. LINEAR TRANSFORMATIONS

1. In mathematics, especially in the area of abstract algebra known as ring theory, a _____ is a ring with 0 ≠ 1 such that ab = 0 implies that either a = 0 or b = 0 (the zero-product property.) That is, it is a nontrivial ring without left or right zero divisors. A commutative _____ is called an integral _____.
    a. Domain
    b. Partially-ordered ring
    c. Subring
    d. Coherent ring

2. In its simplest meaning in mathematics and logic, an _____ is an action or procedure which produces a new value from one or more input values. There are two common types of operations: unary and binary. Unary operations involve only one value, such as negation and trigonometric functions.
    a. AKS primality test
    b. Operation
    c. Abelian P-root group
    d. ADE classification

3. In mathematics the _____ of a set which is equipped with the operation of addition is an element which, when added to any element x in the set, yields x. One of the most familiar additive identities is the number 0 from elementary mathematics, but additive identities occur in other mathematical structures where addition is defined, such as in groups and rings.

    - The _____ familiar from elementary mathematics is zero, denoted 0. For example,

    $5 + 0 = 5 = 0 + 5$.

    - In the natural numbers N and all of its supersets (the integers Z, the rational numbers Q, the real numbers R, or the complex numbers C), the _____ is 0. Thus for any one of these numbers n,

    $n + 0 = n = 0 + n$.

Let N be a set which is closed under the operation of addition, denoted +. An _____ for N is any element e such that for any element n in N,

$e + n = n = n + e$.

   a. Universal algebra
   b. Additive identity
   c. Identity element
   d. External

Chapter 6. LINEAR TRANSFORMATIONS

4. In mathematics, the _____ of a number n is the number that, when added to n, yields zero. The _____ of F is denoted −F.

For example, the _____ of 7 is −7, because 7 + (−7) = 0, and the _____ of −0.3 is 0.3, because −0.3 + 0.3 = 0.

   a. Isomorphism class
   b. Interior algebra
   c. Artinian ideal
   d. Additive inverse

5. _____ is the branch of mathematics concerned with the study of vectors, vector spaces, linear maps, and systems of linear equations. Vector spaces are a central theme in modern mathematics; thus, _____ is widely used in both abstract algebra and functional analysis. _____ also has a concrete representation in analytic geometry and it is generalized in operator theory.
   a. Coordinate vector
   b. Flag
   c. Linear algebra
   d. Schur complement

6. In mathematics, a _____ is a rectangular array of numbers. This way, matrices can record data that depend on multiple parameters. In particular they are used to keep track of the coefficients of multiple linear equations. Matrices are closely connected to linear transformations, which are higher-dimensional analogs of linear functions, i.e., functions of the form f(x) = c Â· x, where c is a constant. This map corresponds to a _____ with one row and column, with entry c. In addition to a number of elementary, entrywise operations such as _____ addition a key notion is _____ multiplication, which displays a number of features not encountered in numbers; for example, products of matrices depend on the order of the factors, unlike products of real numbers, say, where c Â· d = d Â· c for any two numbers c and d.
   a. Polynomial expression
   b. Heap
   c. Commutativity
   d. Matrix

7. In linear algebra and functional analysis, a _____ is a linear transformation P from a vector space to itself such that P² = P. It leaves its image unchanged. Though abstract, this definition of '_____' formalizes and generalizes the idea of graphical _____.

Chapter 6. LINEAR TRANSFORMATIONS

a. Convolution power
b. C_0-semigroup
c. Projection
d. Lumer-Phillips theorem

8. In geometry and linear algebra, a _____ is a transformation in a plane or in space that describes the motion of a rigid body around a fixed point. A _____ is different from a translation, which has no fixed points, and from a reflection, which 'flips' the bodies it is transforming. A _____ and the above-mentioned transformations are isometries; they leave the distance between any two points unchanged after the transformation.

a. Real matrices
b. Reflection
c. Shear mappings
d. Rotation

9. In mathematics, two vectors are _____ if they are perpendicular, i.e., they form a right angle. The word comes from the Greek ά½€ρθïŒς , meaning 'straight', and γωνῖα (gonia), meaning 'angle'. For example, a subway and the street above, although they do not physically intersect, are _____ if they cross at a right angle.

a. Expression
b. Unital
c. Embedding
d. Orthogonal

10. In the various branches of mathematics that fall under the heading of abstract algebra, the _____ of a homomorphism measures the degree to which the homomorphism fails to be injective. An important special case is the _____ of a matrix, also called the null space.

The definition of _____ takes various forms in various contexts.

a. Completing the square
b. Kernel
c. K-theory
d. Monomial basis

11. The column _____ of a matrix A is the maximal number of linearly independent columns of A. Likewise, the row _____ is the maximal number of linearly independent rows of A.

Chapter 6. LINEAR TRANSFORMATIONS

Since the column _____ and the row _____ are always equal, they are simply called the _____ of A. More abstractly, it is the dimension of the image of A. For the proofs, see, e.g., Murase (1960), Andrea ' Wong (1960), Williams ' Cater (1968), Mackiw (1995.) It is commonly denoted by either rk(A) or _____ A.

a. Rank
b. Generalized Pauli matrices
c. Schur complement
d. Split-complex number

12. In abstract algebra, an _____ is a bijective map f such that both f and its inverse f^{-1} are homomorphisms, i.e., structure-preserving mappings. In the more general setting of category theory, an _____ is a morphism f:X→Y in a category for which there exists an 'inverse' f^{-1}:Y→X, with the property that both $f^{-1}f=id_X$ and $ff^{-1}=id_Y$.

Informally, an _____ is a kind of mapping between objects, which shows a relationship between two properties or operations.

a. ADE classification
b. Endomorphism
c. Epimorphism
d. Isomorphism

13. In mathematics, the _____ of a vector space V is the cardinality (i.e. the number of vectors) of a basis of V. It is sometimes called Hamel _____ or algebraic _____ to distinguish it from other types of _____. All bases of a vector space have equal cardinality and so the _____ of a vector space is uniquely defined. The _____ of the vector space V over the field F can be written as $\dim_F(V)$ or as [V : F], read '_____ of V over F'.

a. Partial trace
b. Dual basis
c. Cofactor
d. Dimension

14. In mathematics, a _____ is a function between two vector spaces that preserves the operations of vector addition and scalar multiplication. The expression 'linear operator' is in especially common use, for linear maps from a vector space to itself In advanced mathematics, the definition of linear function coincides with the definition of _____.

Chapter 6. LINEAR TRANSFORMATIONS

a. Homomorphic secret sharing
b. Rotation
c. Real matrices
d. Linear map

15. Let S be a set with a binary operation * . If e is an identity element of (S, *) and a * b = e, then a is called a _____ of b and b is called a right inverse of a. If an element x is both a _____ and a right inverse of y, then x is called a two-sided inverse, or simply an inverse, of y.

   a. -module
   b. 2-bridge knot
   c. -equivalence
   d. Left inverse

16. for some m×n matrix A, called the _____ of T.

Matrices allow arbitrary linear transformations to be represented in a consistent format, suitable for computation. This also allows transformations to be concatenated easily (by multiplying their matrices.)

   a. Transformation matrix
   b. -equivalence
   c. -module
   d. 2-bridge knot

17. In linear algebra, two n-by-n matrices A and B are called _____ if

$$B = P^{-1}AP$$

for some invertible n-by-n matrix P. _____ matrices represent the same linear transformation under two different bases, with P being the change of basis matrix.

The matrix P is sometimes called a similarity transformation. In the context of matrix groups, similarity is sometimes referred to as conjugacy, with _____ matrices being conjugate.

   a. Zero matrix
   b. Similar
   c. Skew-symmetric
   d. Cartan matrix

Chapter 6. LINEAR TRANSFORMATIONS

18. In linear algebra, the _____ of a matrix A is the collection of cells $A_{i,j}$ where i is equal to j.

The _____ of a square matrix is the diagonal which runs from the top left corner to the bottom right corner. For example, the following matrix has 1s down its _____:

$$\begin{bmatrix} 1 & 0 & 0 \\ 0 & 1 & 0 \\ 0 & 0 & 1 \end{bmatrix}.$$

A square matrix like the above in which the entries outside the _____ are all zero is called a diagonal matrix.

a. Diagonalizable matrix
b. Complex Hadamard matrix
c. Polynomial matrix
d. Main diagonal

19. In mathematics, a _____ is a flat surface. Planes can arise as subspaces of some higher dimensional space, as with the walls of a room, or they may enjoy an independent existence in their own right, as in the setting of Euclidean geometry

a. -module
b. Similarity
c. -equivalence
d. Plane

20. In mathematics, an _____ of a product of sums expresses it as a sum of products by using the fact that multiplication distributes over addition. Expansions of polynomials are obtained by multiplying together their factors, which results in a sum of terms with variables raised to different degrees.

To multiply two factors, each term of the first factor must be multiplied by each term of the other factor.

a. Ordered vector space
b. Analytic subgroup
c. Equipotential surfaces
d. Expansion

21. In linear algebra, a _____ is a linear transformation that squares to the identity ($R^2 = I$, where R is in K dimensional space), also known as an involution in the general linear group. In addition to reflections across hyperplanes, the class of general reflections includes point reflections, reflections across subspaces of intermediate dimension, and non-orthogonal reflections.

A _____ over a hyperplane in an inner product space is necessarily symmetric, but a general _____ need not be as the example $\begin{bmatrix} 1 & 0 \\ 1 & -1 \end{bmatrix}$ shows.

   a. Homomorphic secret sharing
   b. Shear mappings
   c. Morphism
   d. Reflection

Chapter 7. EIGENVALUES AND EIGENVECTORS

1. For each eigenvector of a linear transformation, there is a corresponding scalar value called an _____ for that vector, which determines the amount the eigenvector is scaled under the linear transformation. For example, an _____ of +2 means that the eigenvector is doubled in length and points in the same direction. An _____ of +1 means that the eigenvector is unchanged, while an _____ of −1 means that the eigenvector is reversed in sense.
    a. Abelian P-root group
    b. Eigenvalue
    c. ADE classification
    d. AKS primality test

2. For each _____ of a linear transformation, there is a corresponding scalar value called an eigenvalue for that vector, which determines the amount the _____ is scaled under the linear transformation. For example, an eigenvalue of +2 means that the _____ is doubled in length and points in the same direction. An eigenvalue of +1 means that the _____ is unchanged, while an eigenvalue of −1 means that the _____ is reversed in sense.
    a. ADE classification
    b. AKS primality test
    c. Abelian P-root group
    d. Eigenvector

3. In mathematics, a _____ is a rectangular array of numbers. This way, matrices can record data that depend on multiple parameters. In particular they are used to keep track of the coefficients of multiple linear equations. Matrices are closely connected to linear transformations, which are higher-dimensional analogs of linear functions, i.e., functions of the form f(x) = c · x, where c is a constant. This map corresponds to a _____ with one row and column, with entry c. In addition to a number of elementary, entrywise operations such as _____ addition a key notion is _____ multiplication, which displays a number of features not encountered in numbers; for example, products of matrices depend on the order of the factors, unlike products of real numbers, say, where c · d = d · c for any two numbers c and d.
    a. Matrix
    b. Heap
    c. Commutativity
    d. Polynomial expression

4. In mathematics, the _____ of a ring R, often denoted char(R), is defined to be the smallest number of times one must add the ring's multiplicative identity element (1) to itself to get the additive identity element (0); the ring is said to have _____ zero if this repeated sum never reaches the additive identity. That is, char(R) is the smallest positive number n such that

$$\underbrace{1 + \cdots + 1}_{n \text{ summands}} = 0$$

if such a number n exists, and 0 otherwise. The _____ may also be taken to be the exponent of the ring's additive group, that is, the smallest positive n such that

$$\underbrace{a + \cdots + a}_{n \text{ summands}} = 0$$

for every element a of the ring (again, if n exists; otherwise zero.)

    a. Coherent ring
    b. Hereditary
    c. Characteristic
    d. Free ideal ring

5. In discrete mathematics, the _____ is used when solving recurrence problems. One can specify a recurrence relation of the form

$$t_n = At_{n-1} + Bt_{n-2}$$

where the value of t_n is dependent on the values of t_{n-1} and t_{n-2}. When solving a recurrence relation, the goal is to eliminate this dependency and derive an equation of the form

$$t_n = c_1 r_1^{n} + c_2 r_2^{n},$$

where c_1 and c_2 are constants and r_1 and r_2 are the roots of the _____

$$r^2 - Ar - B = 0,$$

where A and B are the constants defined in the original recurrence relation.

    a. Characteristic equation
    b. -module
    c. 2-bridge knot
    d. -equivalence

6. In linear algebra, one associates a polynomial to every square matrix, its _____. This polynomial encodes several important properties of the matrix, most notably its eigenvalues, its determinant and its trace.

Chapter 7. EIGENVALUES AND EIGENVECTORS

Given a square matrix A, we want to find a polynomial whose roots are precisely the eigenvalues of A. For a diagonal matrix A, the _____ is easy to define: if the diagonal entries are a_1, a_2, a_3, etc.

a. Constant term
b. Characteristic polynomial
c. Square-free polynomial
d. Quasi-polynomial

7. In the mathematical discipline of linear algebra, a _____ is a special kind of square matrix where the entries either below or above the main diagonal are zero. Because matrix equations with triangular matrices are easier to solve they are very important in numerical analysis. The LU decomposition gives an algorithm to decompose any invertible matrix A into a normed lower triangle matrix L and an upper triangle matrix U.
    a. Hilbert matrix
    b. Circulant matrix
    c. Diagonally dominant
    d. Triangular matrix

8. In mathematics, a _____ is a function between two vector spaces that preserves the operations of vector addition and scalar multiplication. The expression 'linear operator' is in especially common use, for linear maps from a vector space to itself In advanced mathematics, the definition of linear function coincides with the definition of _____.
    a. Real matrices
    b. Rotation
    c. Linear map
    d. Homomorphic secret sharing

9. In mathematics, an element x of a ring R is called _____ if there exists some positive integer n such that $x^n = 0$.

The term was introduced by Benjamin Peirce in the context of elements of an algebra that vanish when raised to a power.

- This definition can be applied in particular to square matrices. The matrix

$$A = \begin{pmatrix} 0 & 1 & 0 \\ 0 & 0 & 1 \\ 0 & 0 & 0 \end{pmatrix}$$

is _____ because $A^3 = 0$. See _____ matrix for more.

a. Product ring
b. Ring of integers
c. Hochschild homology
d. Nilpotent

10. In linear algebra, two n-by-n matrices A and B are called _____ if

$$B = P^{-1}AP$$

for some invertible n-by-n matrix P. _____ matrices represent the same linear transformation under two different bases, with P being the change of basis matrix.

The matrix P is sometimes called a similarity transformation. In the context of matrix groups, similarity is sometimes referred to as conjugacy, with _____ matrices being conjugate.

a. Cartan matrix
b. Zero matrix
c. Skew-symmetric
d. Similar

11. In linear algebra, a square matrix A is called diagonalizable if it is similar to a diagonal matrix, i.e., if there exists an invertible matrix P such that $P^{-1}AP$ is a diagonal matrix. If V is a finite-dimensional vector space, then a linear map T : V → V is called diagonalizable if there exists a basis of V with respect to which T is represented by a diagonal matrix. Diagonalization is the process of finding a corresponding diagonal matrix for a _____ or linear map.

a. Cauchy matrix
b. Diagonalizable Matrix
c. Pascal matrix
d. Hamiltonian matrix

12. In linear algebra, the _____ of a matrix A is the collection of cells $A_{i,j}$ where i is equal to j.

The _____ of a square matrix is the diagonal which runs from the top left corner to the bottom right corner. For example, the following matrix has 1s down its _____:

$$\begin{bmatrix} 1 & 0 & 0 \\ 0 & 1 & 0 \\ 0 & 0 & 1 \end{bmatrix}.$$

Chapter 7. EIGENVALUES AND EIGENVECTORS

A square matrix like the above in which the entries outside the _____ are all zero is called a diagonal matrix.

a. Polynomial matrix
b. Diagonalizable matrix
c. Complex Hadamard matrix
d. Main diagonal

13. In propositional logic, a set of Boolean operators is called _____ if it permits the realisation of any possible truth table.

Example truth table (Xor):

Using a complete Boolean algebra which does not include XOR (such as the well-known AND OR NOT set), this function can be realised as follows:

(a or b) and not (a and b.)

However, other complete Boolean algebras are possible, such as NAND or NOR (either gate can form a complete Boolean algebra by itself - the proof is detailed on their pages.)

a. Two-element Boolean algebra
b. Sufficient
c. Symmetric Boolean function
d. Complete Boolean algebra

14. In mathematics, particularly linear algebra and functional analysis, the _____ is any of a number of results about linear operators or about matrices. In broad terms the _____ provides conditions under which an operator or a matrix can be diagonalized (that is, represented as a diagonal matrix in some basis.) This concept of diagonalization is relatively straightforward for operators on finite-dimensional spaces, but requires some modification for operators on infinite-dimensional spaces.

a. Spectral radius
b. Spectral asymmetry
c. Spectral geometry
d. Spectral Theorem

15. In abstract algebra and algebraic geometry, the _____ of a commutative ring R, denoted by Spec(R), is the set of all proper prime ideals of R. It is commonly augmented with the Zariski topology and with a structure sheaf, turning it into a locally ringed space.

Spec(R) can be turned into a topological space as follows: a subset V of Spec(R) is closed if and only if there exists a subset I of R such that V consists of all those prime ideals in R that contain I. This is called the Zariski topology on Spec(R.)

Spec(R) is a compact space, but almost never Hausdorff: in fact, the maximal ideals in R are precisely the closed points in this topology.

a. Discrete valuation
b. Hilbert polynomial
c. Spectrum
d. Krull dimension

16. The set of all symmetry operations considered, on all objects in a set X, can be modeled as a group action g : G × X → X, where the image of g in G and x in X is written as gÂ·x. If, for some g, gÂ·x = y then x and y are said to be symmetrical to each other. For each object x, operations g for which gÂ·x = x form a group, the _____ of the object, a subgroup of G. If the _____ of x is the trivial group then x is said to be asymmetric, otherwise symmetric.

a. 2-bridge knot
b. Symmetry group
c. -equivalence
d. -module

17. In linear algebra, a _____ is a square matrix, A, that is equal to its transpose

$$A = A^T.$$

The entries of a _____ are symmetric with respect to the main diagonal (top left to bottom right.) So if the entries are written as A = (a_{ij}), then

$$a_{ij} = a_{ji}$$

for all indices i and j. The following 3×3 matrix is symmetric:

$$\begin{bmatrix} 1 & 2 & 3 \\ 2 & 4 & -5 \\ 3 & -5 & 6 \end{bmatrix}.$$

A matrix is called skew-symmetric or antisymmetric if its transpose is the same as its negative.

a. Butson-type
b. Zero matrix
c. Stieltjes matrix
d. Symmetric matrix

18. In mathematics, two vectors are _____ if they are perpendicular, i.e., they form a right angle. The word comes from the Greek ἀ½€ρθϊŒς , meaning 'straight', and γωνῖ α (gonia), meaning 'angle'. For example, a subway and the street above, although they do not physically intersect, are _____ if they cross at a right angle.
   a. Unital
   b. Expression
   c. Embedding
   d. Orthogonal

19. In linear algebra, an _____ is a square matrix with real entries whose columns (or rows) are orthogonal unit vectors (i.e., orthonormal.) Equivalently, a matrix Q is orthogonal if its transpose is equal to its inverse:

$$Q^T Q = Q Q^T = I.$$

As a linear transformation, an _____ preserves the dot product of vectors, and therefore acts as an isometry of Euclidean space, such as a rotation or reflection.

The set of n × n orthogonal matrices forms a group O(n), known as the orthogonal group.

   a. Alternating sign matrix
   b. Orthogonal matrix
   c. Unistochastic matrix
   d. Unimodular matrix

20. Let S be a set with a binary operation * . If e is an identity element of (S, *) and a * b = e, then a is called a _____ of b and b is called a right inverse of a. If an element x is both a _____ and a right inverse of y, then x is called a two-sided inverse, or simply an inverse, of y.
   a. -module
   b. 2-bridge knot
   c. -equivalence
   d. Left inverse

21. A _____ is a mathematical equation for an unknown function of one or several variables that relates the values of the function itself and its derivatives of various orders. Differential equations play a prominent role in engineering, physics, economics and other disciplines. Visualization of airflow into a duct modelled using the Navier-Stokes equations, a set of partial differential equations.

Differential equations arise in many areas of science and technology; whenever a deterministic relationship involving some continuously changing quantities (modeled by functions) and their rates of change (expressed as derivatives) is known or postulated.

   a. -equivalence
   b. -module
   c. 2-bridge knot
   d. Differential equation

22. In mathematics, a _____ is a homogeneous polynomial of degree two in a number of variables. For example,

$$4x^2 + 2xy - 3y^2$$

is a _____ in the variables x and y.

Quadratic forms are central objects in mathematics, occurring for instance in number theory, geometry (Riemannian metric), topology (intersection forms on homology), and Lie theory (the Killing form.)

   a. Quadratic form
   b. Partial trace
   c. Rank
   d. Homogeneous coordinates

23. An _____ is a type of quadric surface that is a higher dimensional analogue of an ellipse. The equation of a standard axis-aligned _____ body in an xyz-Cartesian coordinate system is

$$\frac{x^2}{a^2} + \frac{y^2}{b^2} + \frac{z^2}{c^2} = 1$$

where a and b are the equatorial radii (along the x and y axes) and c is the polar radius (along the z-axis), all of which are fixed positive real numbers determining the shape of the _____.

More generally, a not-necessarily-axis-aligned _____ is defined by the equation

$$\mathbf{x}^T A \mathbf{x} = 1$$

where A is a symmetric positive definite matrix and x is a vector.

a. Abelian P-root group
b. Ellipsoid
c. ADE classification
d. AKS primality test

24. In mathematics, a _____ is a quadric, a type of surface in three dimensions, described by the equation

$$\frac{x^2}{a^2} + \frac{y^2}{b^2} - \frac{z^2}{c^2} = 1$$

_____ of one sheet,

or

$$-\frac{x^2}{a^2} - \frac{y^2}{b^2} + \frac{z^2}{c^2} = 1$$

_____ of two sheets.

These are also called elliptical hyperboloids. If, and only if, a = b, it is a _____ of revolution, and is also called a circular _____.

a. -module
b. -equivalence
c. Hyperboloid
d. 2-bridge knot

25. The _____ is a doubly ruled surface shaped like a saddle. In a suitable coordinate system, it can be represented by the equation

$$z = \frac{x^2}{a^2} - \frac{y^2}{b^2}.$$

This is a _____ that opens up along the x-axis and down along the y-axis.

Paraboloid of revolution

Chapter 7. EIGENVALUES AND EIGENVECTORS

With a = b an elliptic paraboloid is a paraboloid of revolution: a surface obtained by revolving a parabola around its axis.

a. Hyperbolic paraboloid
b. Prolate spheroid
c. Morin surface
d. Cross-cap

26. In topology, especially algebraic topology, the _____ CX of a topological space X is the quotient space:

$$CX = (X \times I)/(X \times \{0\})$$

of the product of X with the unit interval I = [0, 1]. Intuitively we make X into a cylinder and collapse one end of the cylinder to a point.

If X sits inside Euclidean space, the _____ on X is homeomorphic to the union of lines from X to another point.

a. Descent
b. Genus
c. Cone
d. Smash product

27. In mathematics, a _____ is a quadric surface of special kind. There are two kinds of paraboloids: elliptic and hyperbolic. The elliptic _____ is shaped like an oval cup and can have a maximum or minimum point.

a. Developable surface
b. Paraboloid
c. Focal surface
d. PDE surfaces

28. In linear algebra, the _____ of the monic polynomial

$$p(t) = c_0 + c_1 t + \ldots + c_{n-1} t^{n-1} + t^n$$

Chapter 7. EIGENVALUES AND EIGENVECTORS

is the square matrix defined as

$$C(p) = \begin{bmatrix} 0 & 0 & \cdots & 0 & -c_0 \\ 1 & 0 & \cdots & 0 & -c_1 \\ 0 & 1 & \cdots & 0 & -c_2 \\ \vdots & \vdots & \vdots & \vdots & \vdots \\ 0 & 0 & \cdots & 1 & -c_{n-1} \end{bmatrix}.$$

With this convention, and writing the basis as $v_1, \ldots, v_n$, one has $Cv_i = C^{i-1}v_1 = v_{i+1}$ (for $i < n$), and v_1 generates V as a K[C]-module: C cycles basis vectors.

Some authors use the transpose of this matrix, which (dually) cycles coordinates, and is more convenient for some purposes, like linear recursive relations.

The characteristic polynomial as well as the minimal polynomial of C(p) are equal to p; in this sense, the matrix C(p) is the 'companion' of the polynomial p.

a. Wilkinson matrices
b. Matrix representation
c. Levinson recursion
d. Companion matrix

29. In mathematics and statistics, a _____ or stochastic vector is a vector with non-negative entries that add up to one.

The positions (indices) of a _____ represent the possible outcomes of a discrete random variable, and the vector gives us the probability mass function of that random variable, which is the standard way of characterizing a discrete probability distribution.

Here are some examples of probability vectors:

$$x_0 = \begin{bmatrix} 0.5 \\ 0.25 \\ 0.25 \end{bmatrix}, \quad x_1 = \begin{bmatrix} 0 \\ 1 \\ 0 \end{bmatrix}, \quad x_2 = \begin{bmatrix} 0.65 \\ 0.35 \end{bmatrix}, \quad x_3 = \begin{bmatrix} 0.3 \\ 0.5 \\ 0.07 \\ 0.1 \\ 0.03 \end{bmatrix}.$$

Chapter 7. EIGENVALUES AND EIGENVECTORS

Writing out the vector components of a vector p as

$$p = \begin{bmatrix} p_1 \\ p_2 \\ \vdots \\ p_n \end{bmatrix}$$

the vector components must sum to one:

$$\sum_{i=1}^{n} p_i = 1$$

One also has the requirement that each individual component must have a probability between zero and one:

$$0 \leq p_i \leq 1$$

for all i.

- a. -equivalence
- b. -module
- c. 2-bridge knot
- d. Probability vector

30. The real component of a quaternion is also called its _____ part.

The term is also sometimes used informally to mean a vector, matrix, tensor, or other usually 'compound' value that is actually reduced to a single component. Thus, for example, the product of a 1×n matrix and an n×1 matrix, which is formally a 1×1 matrix, is often said to be a _____.

- a. Tensor product
- b. Self-adjoint
- c. Distributivity
- d. Scalar

31. In mathematics, _____ is one of the basic operations defining a vector space in linear algebra Note that _____ is different from scalar product which is an inner product between two vectors.

More specifically, if K is a field and V is a vector space over K, then _____ is a function from K × V to V. The result of applying this function to c in K and v in V is denoted cv.

a. Symplectic vector space
b. Scalar multiplication
c. K-frame
d. Matrix pencil

ANSWER KEY

Chapter 1
1. d 2. c 3. d 4. a 5. d 6. b 7. c 8. c 9. c 10. d
11. a 12. d 13. d 14. d 15. d 16. d

Chapter 2
1. d 2. b 3. d 4. d 5. c 6. d 7. d 8. a 9. d 10. d
11. c 12. d 13. a 14. d 15. d 16. b 17. d 18. d 19. d 20. d
21. b 22. d 23. c 24. b 25. c 26. a 27. a 28. b 29. d 30. b

Chapter 3
1. d 2. b 3. d 4. b 5. c 6. c 7. d 8. c 9. b 10. d
11. d 12. b 13. a 14. b 15. b 16. a 17. b 18. c 19. d 20. c
21. a 22. c 23. b 24. d 25. a 26. d 27. d 28. d 29. d 30. a
31. a 32. d

Chapter 4
1. d 2. d 3. d 4. d 5. d 6. d 7. c 8. d 9. c 10. d
11. a 12. b 13. c 14. d 15. d 16. d 17. d 18. d 19. c 20. b
21. c 22. a 23. d 24. d 25. d 26. b 27. c 28. a 29. c 30. a
31. b 32. d 33. a 34. c 35. a

Chapter 5
1. d 2. d 3. d 4. b 5. b 6. c 7. c 8. d 9. d 10. c
11. d 12. c 13. c 14. d 15. b 16. a 17. b 18. c 19. a 20. c
21. d 22. a 23. a 24. d 25. d 26. c 27. c 28. d 29. b 30. c
31. d 32. d 33. d

Chapter 6
1. a 2. b 3. b 4. d 5. c 6. d 7. c 8. d 9. d 10. b
11. a 12. d 13. d 14. d 15. d 16. a 17. b 18. d 19. d 20. d
21. d

Chapter 7
1. b 2. d 3. a 4. c 5. a 6. b 7. d 8. c 9. d 10. d
11. b 12. d 13. b 14. d 15. c 16. b 17. d 18. d 19. b 20. d
21. d 22. a 23. b 24. c 25. a 26. c 27. b 28. d 29. d 30. d
31. b

www.ingramcontent.com/pod-product-compliance
Lightning Source LLC
Chambersburg PA
CBHW081849230426
43669CB00018B/2879